CANCER
2003

CANCER
2003

Jane Struthers

p

This is a Parragon Book
First published in 2002

Parragon
Queen Street House
4 Queen Street
Bath BA1 1HE
UK

Produced by Magpie Books, an imprint of
Constable & Robinson Ltd, London

© Jane Struthers 2002

Illustrations courtesy of Slatter-Anderson, London
Cover courtesy of Simon Levy

ISBN 0-75258-671-8

A copy of the British Library Cataloguing-in-Publication Data
is available from the British Library

Printed and bound in the EC

CONTENTS

Dates for 2003

Cancer 22 June – 22 July

Leo 23 July – 23 August

Virgo 24 August – 23 September

Libra 24 September – 23 October

Scorpio 24 October – 22 November

Sagittarius 23 November – 21 December

Capricorn 22 December – 20 January

Aquarius 21 January – 18 February

Pisces 19 February – 20 March

Aries 21 March – 20 April

Taurus 21 April – 21 May

Gemini 22 May – 21 June

INTRODUCTION

Dear Cancer

Happy 2003! I hope you have a fantastic year with the aid of this book. It's designed to help you make the most of the highlights and steer yourself quickly through the low points.

If you can't wait to find out what 2003 holds for you, turn immediately to **The Year 2003**, my summary of what you can expect in your relationships, health, money and career. My day by day forecasts for 2003 follow on, with at-a-glance charts that give you the general flavour of each month.

Your Cancer Sun Sign is full of information about what makes you tick, and particularly about how you operate in four areas of your life: relationships, health, money and career. If you've recently met someone new and you want to know whether your signs hit it off, turn to **Love and the Stars** to find out what astrology says about your relationship. It's a quick guide to your compatibility with each of the twelve signs, and is followed by two charts that show how you get on with the other signs in love and sex, and also in friendship.

Speaking of friendship, how important are friends to you? **Family and Friends** will give you the answers and also reveal what you really think about your family. Do you simply tolerate them or are they the centre of your world?

If you've never been sure whether you're Gemini, Cancer or Leo because you were born at the start or end of Cancer, **Born on the Cusp?** will solve the problem once and for all.

Once you've read all that you'll be thoroughly equipped for 2003, so enjoy it!

Jane Struthers

THE YEAR 2003

 Friends and Lovers

Close relationships have puzzled you over recent years and they'll continue to perplex you at times in 2003. You may have to deal with a partner who blows hot and cold so you never know entirely where you stand and whether you're in favour or in trouble. If you've had a lot of this treatment from a certain person recently you may now decide that you've got to do something about it, but try not to rush into rash decisions. Think things through carefully and then take action. There's also a chance that you'll try to turn a blind eye to what's going on in the hope that it will all blow over, but bear in mind that it may not do so and you'll have to do something about it eventually.

If the atmosphere has sometimes been dicey with neighbours, close relatives and other people who you see on an almost daily basis, you'll get a chance to improve the situation from late August onwards. It may help to introduce an element of humour into what's going on, without giving the impression that you're laughing at anyone. Talking things through will be another good way to resolve any problems between you. After all, if you don't discuss things you won't know what each of you thinks.

The world seems a much more serious place than usual from early June, and this could have an impact on your relationships. For instance, you may be drawn to people who reflect your own earnest or solemn ideas or who are intellectual heavyweights. All the same, try to mix with people who make you laugh as well – otherwise you could end up feeling rather bogged down.

Health

There has been a lot of emphasis on your health during the past few years and you'll still need to pay attention to it in 2003. Don't be tempted to neglect or ignore any strange symptoms or ailments that affect you because you'll only worry about them. It will be far better to put your mind at rest by seeking medical advice. You may well find you were worrying about nothing.

This is an excellent year to detoxify your system in some way. You might decide to have a month off all booze, to give yourself a break from cigarettes, to stop drinking coffee, to give up chocolate, or to do anything else that seems like a good idea. You could feel completely refreshed and renewed if you stick with it.

If you're a typical Cancerian you have a strong tendency to worry about things. This is especially likely in the first half of the year, when anxieties will prey on your mind if you let them and then start to affect your health in some way. Try not to let this happen if you can possibly avoid it: it won't do you any good.

Keeping active and busy will help to combat any anxieties that do affect you. You'll especially enjoy being involved in neighbourhood issues and local concerns, and you'll also get a lot of pleasure out of taking walks in the countryside or in other beautiful surroundings. It will be a great way to unwind.

Money

The good news is that your finances are looking rosy at the start of the year and your financial climate will continue to be very favourable until the end of August. This is a marvellous chance to make investments, whether big or small, and generally to put your money to good use. Although a little speculation could pay off surprisingly well and be amazingly lucky, you should be very wary of gambling with anything that you can't afford to lose.

The first eight months of the year are fantastic for schemes that will enable your money to grow. You might decide to put regular amounts into a savings account or to buy items that you hope will be a good investment, such as jewellery or paintings. However, steer clear of any schemes that make unrealistic promises or could lead to big losses. Luck is on your side up to a point now but you won't be infallible. You should also be wary of investing in dodgy or shady deals or projects in case they backfire on you and you lose your investment.

If you're pooling your resources with someone else, one of you might have a change of heart or not be entirely straightforward about what's going on, so be careful.

Career

If you want to make a success of your career this year, improve your communications as much as possible. This is especially important from late August but it will also matter before then. You might decide to buy a new computer, upgrade your mobile phone or learn a new skill that enables you to connect with others. Any work that involves writing or talking will go well, and you'll be riding high if your job is connected with buying and selling, advertising or market research.

Your sense of duty and responsibility is heightened from early June and there will be times when you're prepared to burn the midnight oil if that's what it takes to do a good job. Although this will be very impressive, don't overdo it or you won't be able to perform at your best. So make sure you get plenty of breaks and don't neglect your social life.

If you aren't happy with your current job or working conditions but haven't yet done anything about them, now is the time to swing into action. You may feel that it's a case of all or nothing, yet be powerless to introduce such radical change into your life. If so, allow yourself to make a series of small alterations that will build up into something much bigger, given time. You should also fight against any feelings of powerlessness that may swamp you, and do your best to retain some control of the situation, and certainly of the way you react to it. In other words, don't let people bully you!

Your Day by Day Guide

JANUARY AT A GLANCE

Love	♥ ♥ ♥ ♥ ♥
Money	£ $ £ $ £
Career	💻 💻 💻 💻
Health	☼ ☼ ☼ ☼

• *Wednesday 1 January* •

Even if you were up half the night celebrating the arrival of 2003, you're still feeling optimistic and cheerful today. It's a super start to the new year and you're in confident mood. The most enjoyable way to spend the day is doing things that have a lot of meaning for you and which make you feel good too. You might also consider doing something that boosts your physical health.

• *Thursday 2 January* •

Today's New Moon sets the tone for the coming fortnight because it places the accent firmly on your relationships. If a partnership has been languishing in the doldrums recently, now is the time to do something constructive about it. Maybe you should have a heart-to-heart with the person concerned, so you can work together to find some sort of compromise?

• *Friday 3 January* •

If you're a typical Cancerian you have a strong need to keep tabs on loved ones and you also require plenty of emotional reassurance from them. However, this is guaranteed to get someone's back up today, leading to some tricky scenes from them and hurt feelings on your part. Do your best to give people as much freedom and scope as they need, because clinging to them today will make them want to run off in the opposite direction as fast as possible.

• *Saturday 4 January* •

If you want to understand someone, talk to them today. Try to make it a conversation rather than a monologue, so you get the most out of the encounter. If you have things to get off your chest, don't be afraid to say them. However, it might be a good idea to phrase your words carefully. Try to avoid any implications of blame or resentment, and stick to the facts.

• *Sunday 5 January* •

The atmosphere has lightened considerably and you're feeling much more relaxed today. Perhaps yesterday's conversation has improved things with a certain person or maybe you simply feel relieved at finally having cleared the air. This is a wonderful day for enjoying being with other people, and you can bet that they'll enjoy being with you too.

• *Monday 6 January* •

Someone's in a very emotional mood today and it won't take much to set them off. They might become highly sentimental or even tearful, which could be slightly embarrassing but is unlikely to cause any problems. Women are especially likely to behave like this, particularly if they're feeling rather vulnerable or unsure of themselves.

• *Tuesday 7 January* •

You have a tremendous interest in other people today and you really want to know what makes them tick. It's the perfect excuse for getting together with someone you don't know very well at the moment but who you hope will become a friend in due course. If you need to patch up an argument with you-know-who, make the first move now because they're probably in a conciliatory mood.

• *Wednesday 8 January* •

You long for a mini adventure today! It doesn't have to be very dramatic or daredevil, just as long as it gets your adrenalin going and gives you something new to think about. If you're suffering from an anti-climax after all the recent festivities, consider arranging something that you can look forward to. A holiday or some long-distance travel would be perfect, provided you can afford it.

• *Thursday 9 January* •

You're in a very feisty mood today and are perfectly able to stand up for yourself when necessary. What's more, you'll do this in a good-humoured and jovial way, yet you'll still get your point across. It's also a great day for talking someone round to seeing things from your viewpoint. Your evident enthusiasm will be far more effective than any amount of heavy persuasion.

• *Friday 10 January* •

The atmosphere with a certain person is a bit dicey today. Perhaps they're throwing their weight around or you're being rather overbearing. Rather than heap blame on the other person, try to accept that it's probably six of one and half a dozen of the other. Any resentments that have been lurking in the background are likely to rise to the surface now, giving you the chance to deal with them at long last.

• *Saturday 11 January* •

Someone is very chatty today. They're happy to yak about whatever pops into their head, whether you want to hear about it or not. Although you'll enjoy having a short conversation, you may wish to draw the line at having your ear bent for hours on end. However, bear in mind that you may also be rather verbose right now!

• *Sunday 12 January* •

Any suggestion of possessiveness or jealousy will turn off loved ones faster than a tap today. They have a strong need to go their own way right now and will soon become very impatient if they think you're trying to restrict them or tie them down. Let them do their own thing even if it pains you, because if you don't they're likely to rebel in ways that will be even more disruptive and hurtful in the long run.

• *Monday 13 January* •

You're the soul of diplomacy today, so make the most of it! It's a fantastic day for getting on the right side of someone, especially if they're usually a very difficult customer. For some reason, they're being as sweet as pie today – or as sweet as they can manage without undergoing a complete personality change. Social events will be highly enjoyable and you might even make a new friend as a result.

• *Tuesday 14 January* •

Are you the sort of Cancerian who eats for comfort? If so, you'll be making lots of trips to the fridge or biscuit tin today because you're feeling rather vulnerable and unsure of yourself. Instead of eating yourself into a stupor, try to work out what's wrong and then find a way to fix it. Simply admitting that you're unhappy, rather than blotting out the feeling with some food, will make you feel more in control of things.

• *Wednesday 15 January* •

The voice of conscience is nagging away at you today, making you squirm around like a worm on a pin. You're being very strict with yourself and if you think you've done something wrong you won't let yourself off the hook without a struggle. You may even give yourself a really hard time about it, but what will that achieve in the long run? Far better to learn from your mistake and try to remedy it if possible.

• *Thursday 16 January* •

Have you noticed the sexual chemistry that's buzzing between you and a certain someone today? This person may be your other half, in which case you'll have no qualms about acting on it. But what should you do if you're feeling attracted to someone who's off limits for some reason? Can you enjoy the flirtation because it's harmless fun, or do you suspect that it's leading you into a hot and heavy relationship?

• *Friday 17 January* •

Are you feeling fit and healthy or do you feel sluggish and flabby? The next few weeks are ideal for increasing the amount of exercise you take each day, even if you simply do that by walking round the block each morning or hopping on your bike instead of getting in the car every now and then. Try to find a sensible regime that you can stick to, rather than setting yourself impossible goals and then feeling bad when you inevitably fall short of meeting them.

• *Saturday 18 January* •

The coming fortnight will be a very important time for you, thanks to today's Full Moon. This is your chance to take yourself in hand if needs be and to clear the decks of anything or anyone that no longer belongs in your life, ready for some fresh growth to follow. Forget about clinging on to situations through sheer habit or laziness – be bold enough to set them aside and trust that something better will soon fill the gap.

• *Sunday 19 January* •

Money burns a big hole in your pocket today, so watch out! If the shops are open you'll be there in a flash and spending lavishly, whether that means buying some chocolates with your Sunday newspaper or going into your favourite shop and treating yourself to some irresistible bargains in the January sales. You have a strong need to indulge yourself but try not to bankrupt yourself in the process.

• *Monday 20 January* •

Between now and this time next month you'll want to get much more involved in life than usual. Skimming the surface and dealing with superficialities won't appeal in the slightest, and instead you'll want to immerse yourself in emotión. You might even become interested in life and death issues or want to explore ideas that are usually considered taboo or too risqué to mention in polite company.

• *Tuesday 21 January* •

You're blessed with tremendous generosity of spirit today, as everyone around you will quickly discover. If you're at work, you'll want your colleagues to share in your good mood, perhaps by buying everyone some chocolate biscuits or taking them out for a drink. To put the icing on the cake, you might hear some good news about your job prospects or a forthcoming pay rise.

• *Wednesday 22 January* •

Be choosy about who you confide in today because your words may fall on stony ground. For instance, you might pour your heart out to someone who then makes it clear that they aren't interested or who takes the opportunity to tick you off about what you've said. This isn't what you need at all and it will make you feel utterly wretched. You may decide that your best bet is to confide in your diary or journal.

• *Thursday 23 January* •

You're the apple of someone's eye today and you'll bask in the warmth of their affection. What's more, you're very happy to return the compliment. Why not give someone a hug on the spur of the moment or pay them a heartfelt compliment? Your love and generosity will really touch them and it might even bring you closer together. Don't be shy about showing your feelings!

• *Friday 24 January* •

You revel in your home comforts today and will love doing things that make you feel cosy and safe. For instance, you might decide to stay in tonight and relax, or to gather some of your nearest and dearest around you. If you work from home, this is a super day to make your work space more comfortable and attractive. How about buying yourself a nice cushion to sit on or a picture to hang above your desk?

• *Saturday 25 January* •

You've had problems this month with possessiveness and it rears its ugly head again today. Rather than try to pretend that nothing's wrong, it will be much better to get things out into the open and thrash out your differences with the person concerned. However, do your best to avoid assigning blame, indulging in emotional blackmail or making anyone feel sorry for you because that won't improve the situation one bit.

• *Sunday 26 January* •

If you've been wondering how to improve your job prospects this year, put on your thinking cap today. Your self-confidence is boosted right now and you may decide that you're capable of a lot more than you've given yourself credit for in the past. Maybe this is your cue to branch out in a different direction or apply for a job that will be challenging but enjoyable.

• *Monday 27 January* •

Pay attention to your working environment today. Perhaps it's time you tidied your desk, cleared out your files or did some housekeeping on your computer. It may also be about time that you sorted out a problem with a colleague or simply made more of an effort to get on well with them. The more energy you put into things today, the more you'll gain as a result.

• *Tuesday 28 January* •

How much attention do you pay to your health? If you usually take it for granted, maybe it's time you took it more seriously? This is a fabulous day for spending money on improving your mental and physical well-being. For instance, you might decide to join a gym or sports club if you fancy taking more exercise, or maybe you're interested in adding more organic food to your diet. Any improvements are money well spent now.

• *Wednesday 29 January* •

Take care today because you're very susceptible to the atmosphere around you. To make matters worse, someone is being frosty or remote and your immediate reaction will be to think it's all your fault. The busier or more tired someone is, the more likely they are to give you the brush-off now. Try not to take it to heart unless you're absolutely certain that it's intended to be personal and hurtful.

• *Thursday 30 January* •

Practising a little self-analysis today will have some fantastic effects on you. It might reveal some psychological traps that you keep falling into, or it may show you why you behave in a certain way sometimes. You may even realize that you're fed up with some of your patterns of behaviour and that you're ready to abandon them for something more constructive. You'll amaze yourself!

• *Friday 31 January* •

Your emotions are easily affected today and you may even feel as though you've got a layer of skin missing. This will make you feel very involved with life because you're experiencing it in such an acute way. It's a wonderful day for opening your heart to a loved one, especially if you can do it in private. You'll miss out on a lot now if you ignore or censor your feelings.

FEBRUARY AT A GLANCE

Love	♥ ♥ ♥ ♥ ♥
Money	£ $ £ $ £
Career	💻 💻 💻
Health	☼ ☼ ☼

• *Saturday 1 February* •

Make the effort to get closer to loved ones over the coming fortnight. Not only will you enrich your relationships, you'll also gain a greater understanding of what makes each other tick. If you're currently a single Cancerian, all that could change any minute now when you meet someone who completely bowls you over and captures your heart. Keep your eyes peeled for them!

• *Sunday 2 February* •

Take care when doing anything financial today because it will be awfully easy to get overconfident and imagine that you have a bigger fund at your disposal than is really the case. Alternatively, you may have to deal with someone who is happy to spend your money for you and who won't listen to reason. Nevertheless, you'll thoroughly enjoy parting with your cash whenever you get the chance!

• *Monday 3 February* •

Feeling hard-done-by? It certainly seems that way, especially if you're slogging your guts out for little or no reward. Perhaps everyone is taking you for granted or they've forgotten to praise you for your efforts. You may even have to encroach on your own time in order to complete a task, and you certainly won't be happy about that. But what is the alternative?

• *Tuesday 4 February* •

Between now and early March you'll want to do your utmost
to keep partners happy. The very thought of someone being
annoyed with you will be enough to make you want to bend
over backwards to pacify them. Now, although this means
you'll strive to create harmony, it may also mean that you'll
put your own needs second for the sake of keeping the peace.
There may be times when this is perfectly justified but there
may also be others when you're setting a difficult precedent,
so be careful.

• *Wednesday 5 February* •

You're putting a lot of effort into your work today and you're
busy keeping yourself up to the mark. You may even set
yourself ambitious goals and then be delighted when you
meet them. This is certainly a great day to push yourself
further than usual because you'll take it all in your stride.
You're also interested in taking lots of exercise but don't
overdo it and make yourself ill.

• *Thursday 6 February* •

If you're currently considering making some financial decisions, this is a super day to consult an expert. You're amenable
to what they have to say, and they're prepared to give you the
benefit of the doubt. It's also a good opportunity to talk to
someone whose opinion or experience you respect, and who
can point you in the right direction or give you food for
thought.

• *Friday 7 February* •

Someone's got rather a sharp tongue today, as you discover to
your cost. They may come out with some Smart aleck remarks

that have a sting in the tail or which sound as though they should be jokes but are really put-downs. But before you point the finger of blame at others, bear in mind that you may also be guilty of giving someone a tongue-lashing now. Apologize once you realize what you've done.

• *Saturday 8 February* •

If you fancy making some changes to your life, swing into action today while you're in the mood. As a Cancerian, you aren't always keen on altering the status quo, and there are times when it even seems positively threatening, but you're perfectly prepared to do so right now. Changes connected with your job, health or finances are especially pertinent at the moment and are well worth considering.

• *Sunday 9 February* •

A certain person is being very touchy today and you'll have to tiptoe around them on egg shells if you're to avoid getting it in the neck. But even then you might fall foul of them for some strange reason. If you can sense trouble brewing it will be far better to sort it out sooner rather than later. Remember this if you can feel yourself getting all steamed up. Say what's wrong before you blow a gasket!

• *Monday 10 February* •

Is you-know-who going out of their way to drive you batty or is it unintentional? Either way, your patience is wearing thin and it won't take much to make you stamp your feet and yell your head off today. To make matters worse, one of you feels that your relationship has got stuck in a rut and wants to introduce some innovative changes, while the other is determined to stand their ground. Stalemate!

• *Tuesday 11 February* •

There's only one way to resolve the current conflicts in a relationship and that's to talk about them. Shoving them under the carpet or hoping they'll go away of their own accord will only store up trouble for later on, so find the courage to confront you-know-who and persuade them to discuss what's wrong. Together, you'll be able to find compromises. Apart, you'll just be on a collision course.

• *Wednesday 12 February* •

Give yourself a treat and spend time with a special person today. They'll help to soothe your feelings and will give you something else to think about. Another antidote to the current stress you're experiencing is to forget about your own troubles and concentrate on someone else's. Any form of voluntary or charity work, for instance, will soon remind you to count your blessings.

• *Thursday 13 February* •

It's time to start scrutinizing your finances, especially if you've been neglecting them recently. If you overspent last December and haven't yet caught up, maybe it's time to seek expert advice or to impose a strict budget on yourself. The next few weeks are also a golden opportunity to research your best options for pensions, insurance and other financial provisions for the future.

• *Friday 14 February* •

Today is a wonderful opportunity to go over projects that you've already got off the ground and to check that they're running smoothly. It's also excellent for re-evaluating situations that you're involved in and deciding what action to take next. However, you won't get anywhere if you try to start anything new today because nothing will come of it. Bide your time until tomorrow.

• *Saturday 15 February* •

The more time you devote to people and activities that have a lot of meaning for you, the happier you'll be. In fact, they will do your heart good. They will also remind you of your priorities in life and perhaps make you want to devote more time to them in the future. On a more mundane note, you'll really enjoy spending some money today, especially if you indulge yourself in some way.

• *Sunday 16 February* •

Financial considerations are never far from your thoughts at the moment and today's Full Moon is reminding you about those loose ends that are waiting to be tied up. Sort them out soon because then you can put them out of your mind and concentrate on other things. If you're thinking of selling a possession, the coming fortnight is the perfect time to do it.

• *Monday 17 February* •

You're very sure of yourself today and have made up your mind about something. As far as you're concerned, you've reached a decision and you're going to stick to it. However, as far as others are concerned, you're being stubborn and obstinate, and are refusing to accept any sort of compromise. You won't get anywhere by battling it out today, except to become more entrenched in your views than ever.

• *Tuesday 18 February* •

It's one of those delightful days when it's easy to get on well with whoever happens to be around. You're blessed with tact and diplomacy, and will manage to say the right thing at the right time. Neighbourhood and local events are enjoyable. Even people who aren't always very easy are much more amenable today, so it's a good opportunity to talk to them.

• *Wednesday 19 February* •

Your horizons open up during the coming four weeks, making you eager to explore the world in new ways. Any form of travel, whether physical or mental, is ideal for you now because it will introduce you to new experiences and fresh encounters. If you haven't yet planned your next holiday, it will be almost impossible to stop yourself from visiting your nearest travel agent without delay!

• *Thursday 20 February* •

You're in a very hard-working mood today and want to get a lot done. However, things may not go as planned, resulting in enormous frustration and a sense that you're battling against impossible odds. For instance, someone who is supposed to help you may turn out to be a hindrance instead, or a piece of equipment may go on the blink just at the crucial moment. You can only do your best.

• *Friday 21 February* •

Be very wary about getting involved in official finances today because the picture isn't nearly as clear as it seems. Someone may have forgotten to furnish you with a few vital facts, or perhaps they're deliberately withholding information. You may also be feeling confused and, as a result, are likely to make the wrong decision. Try to wait a couple of days before doing anything decisive or binding.

• Saturday 22 February •

There's a wonderfully convivial atmosphere today and it's making you want to be as sociable as possible. If you don't have anything planned, change that immediately! Invite someone round to your place or arrange to go out on the town with a friend. It's an especially good day for being with your beloved – you'll really appreciate each other's company.

• Sunday 23 February •

Things quickly get on top of you today, making you feel agitated and under pressure. If you're trying to get things done, you may feel that there aren't enough hours in the day or that you're stretching yourself too thin. Take notice of your health because it will be a good barometer of your mental well-being. If you're tense or under a lot of strain, you'll start to feel unwell, which is the signal to take it easy.

• Monday 24 February •

This is a fabulous day for getting things done and you won't relax until you've achieved what you set out to do. This is great if you can keep everything in proportion but you may find that you want to push yourself to the limit or that you're making mountains out of molehills. You may also start to worry about a health problem or an ailment that won't clear up. Seek medical help and put your mind at rest.

• Tuesday 25 February •

If you're at work today you'll get most done if you keep switching jobs. Believe it or not, this will help to maintain your concentration and interest in what you're doing. Slogging away at one thing for hours on end, on the other hand, will soon mean that you get bored and restless. A colleague or customer has something very interesting to say right now, so listen carefully.

• *Wednesday 26 February* •

Tackle any sort of paperwork or red tape today because your eagle eyes won't miss a thing. It's a marvellous day for filling in forms, making applications or doing anything very complicated. This is also a good day for sorting out any health matters that have been puzzling you, perhaps by asking your doctor some tough questions or doing some personal research with the help of books or the Internet.

• *Thursday 27 February* •

Relationships flourish today, helped by everyone's determination to be amenable and helpful. This is just what you need if you've been waiting for the right moment to talk to someone or possibly even ask them a favour. They may not give the response you'd like but at least they'll do it nicely, rather than bite your head off or make you feel as though you're being a nuisance!

• *Friday 28 February* •

You'll get on best if you're able to work by yourself today. Although you aren't feeling antisocial, you don't really want to be surrounded by lots of people either, and will really appreciate having some peace and quiet at some point. When you are with people, it's an excellent opportunity to talk about matters that are very dear to your heart or which you take very seriously, especially if you're choosy about who you discuss them with.

MARCH AT A GLANCE

Love	♥ ♥ ♥ ♥
Money	£ $ £
Career	💻 💻 💻 💻 💻
Health	☼ ☼

• *Saturday 1 March* •

Put on your X-ray specs today because you're capable of some very penetrating insights and thoughts. Instead of glossing over things or making light of them, you want to investigate them in a lot of detail. It's an especially good chance for a heart-to-heart with a partner or close friend, in which you both bare your souls and tell it like it is.

• *Sunday 2 March* •

If your relationship with your other half has started to flag a bit or mundane considerations have meant that all the excitement has gone, the coming four weeks are the ideal chance to breathe new life into it. Maybe you should woo each other all over again or go away for a long weekend so you have some time to yourselves. You need to remind yourselves of why you got together in the first place.

• *Monday 3 March* •

How do you feel about rising to a challenge? During the coming fortnight you could be presented with an exciting chance to prove your worth or show that you've got what it takes. It's also going to be a marvellous opportunity to make you proud of yourself. Any exploits connected with further education, travel, politics, the environment or spirituality all interest you now.

• *Tuesday 4 March* •

Although the accent is on harmonious relationships at the moment, there will be times when they aren't possible. This is especially likely if you're feeling annoyed about someone's behaviour or you've realized that behaving towards them with sweetness and light is only giving them an excuse to carry on treating you badly. When this happens, you'll have to put your foot down and make your feelings known. Be strong, but don't use more force than necessary.

• *Wednesday 5 March* •

There are times when you're quite content to stay at home and not venture far afield, but this isn't one of them! During the coming fortnight you'll thoroughly enjoy spreading your wings and satisfying your current curiosity about the world. You might decide to sign up for a course or class in something that's always fascinated you, or you could become engrossed in a book that leads to a new interest.

• *Thursday 6 March* •

You need some time to yourself today, especially if you're busy working while being surrounded by other people. You have a strong sense of responsibility right now but don't let that make you slog your guts out if you don't have to. A conversation with someone who's older or wiser than you will be very interesting. You may not agree with everything they say but you're both in one mind about most of it.

• *Friday 7 March* •

You're bouncing about like Tigger today, having as good a time as possible. It's a great day for any sort of social event because you're full of self-confidence and want to make a big splash. If you fancy someone and have been waiting for the right moment to start chatting them up, they don't stand a chance today because you're so interesting and dynamic!

• *Saturday 8 March* •

Whatever else you're doing today, try to set aside some time for a hobby or other interest. It will give you a lot of enjoyment, which is always good news, but it will also help you to relax and give you other things to think about besides your everyday concerns. Look on it as a mini holiday! If you're taking part in a group activity now you'll find yourself instinctively dispensing advice or taking charge of things.

• *Sunday 9 March* •

A certain person is being very wilful and determined today, and it means they're making a complete nuisance of themselves. You could easily get drawn into a battle of wills in which neither of you wants to back down or give an inch. You may also find that you're automatically rejecting each other's suggestions without even listening to them, because you're so keen to stand your ground. It'll be exhausting!

• *Monday 10 March* •

Mind how you go when spending money today. You're in the mood to splash it around like water, which is fine if you've got buckets of it but not such good news if you've already encountered a financial drought. And the situation might get worse. However, assuming that you have money to spend, you'll adore buying objects that are fun, luxurious or make you feel good.

• *Tuesday 11 March* •

You have a choice today. You can either respect a certain person's sensibilities and censor almost everything you say to avoid offending them, or you can just open your mouth and blurt out whatever pops into your head. If you follow the latter tactic, however, you should be prepared for a few ructions or even a blazing row. It all depends on the importance of what you have to say.

• *Wednesday 12 March* •

You're completely bewitched by a certain person today and you can't get them out of your mind. You think they're absolutely wonderful and won't hear a word said against them. This is lovely if you're prepared to let reality set in at a later date, but it isn't such good news if you continue to deify this person and imagine that they're superhuman. Be very careful about getting involved in joint financial schemes today because you may not have all the facts at this stage.

• *Thursday 13 March* •

Life is full of opportunities today and you can't wait to get your hands on them. This is no time to expect things to land in your lap without any effort on your part, so be prepared to grab whatever comes along and to make your own luck if necessary. It's also a wonderful day for activities that will teach you more about the world or open your mind in some way.

• *Friday 14 March* •

Put any new projects on hold today: you'll get nowhere fast if you try to get them off the ground. Instead, reassess the progress you've made in ventures that are already up and running. Of course, if you're supposed to begin something that you don't want to come to anything, this is the day to get started on it. With luck, it will all fizzle out and you won't have to do it!

• Saturday 15 March •

People are very emotional today and you may end up drying someone's tears or listening to them getting their knickers in a twist. It's nothing to worry about but you should bear it in mind. If you've fallen out with someone recently, this is a marvellous day to patch things up with them. It will be much easier than you imagine, and you'll be glad you did it.

• Sunday 16 March •

Your powers of concentration are ace today. You're able to screen out any distractions that would otherwise prevent you from getting on with the job in hand. It's also a good day for doing things that are fiddly or which require a tremendous amount of manual dexterity. But try to give yourself a break every now and then, otherwise you'll end up feeling exhausted.

• Monday 17 March •

Something is worrying you and it won't leave you alone. It will be horribly easy to allow yourself to brood on what's wrong but that will mean that things go round in your mind until there's absolutely no escape from them. Try to find some constructive outlet for your anxieties, preferably by taking some form of positive action. Even talking to someone will help you to feel better.

• Tuesday 18 March •

You're going to be doing some hard thinking over the next two weeks, especially if the worries that assailed you yesterday haven't gone away yet. Grab the chance, whenever you get it, to mull things over and take a broad view of your current situation. Getting up too close to it will mean you can't see the wood for the trees, and also that you'll get sidetracked by things that may not be very important.

• *Wednesday 19 March* •

This is an excellent day to take a holistic view of your health and general well-being. Are there any ways in which your life is contributing to your health, or lack of it? For instance, if you're unhappy at work or having to cope with other difficult situations, you may not be as fit or healthy as you would like. How can you improve the situation and, in so doing, boost your own fitness?

• *Thursday 20 March* •

You crave lively company today and will be thrilled whenever you're with anyone who's wacky, unusual or slightly shocking. Even if they're normally a bit too much for you, you're strangely attracted to them right now and find them a lot more interesting than usual. This is also a great day for giving yourself a change of scene at some point, especially if that means visiting somewhere for the first time.

• *Friday 21 March* •

Your goals and ambitions get a big boost from today and over the coming month you'll want to get as many achievements under your belt as possible. Some of these may be connected to your career but don't just concentrate on this aspect of your life. How about setting yourself a goal in something more personal, so you have good reason to feel proud?

• *Saturday 22 March* •

You're feeling industrious and hard-working today, and you'll want to do your best at whatever you tackle. If you're at work, you'll want to pull out the stops. You'll also enjoy a good rapport with colleagues and customers. If you're at home, it's a good day for talking to people whose opinions and experience you respect and who have something valuable to teach you.

• *Sunday 23 March* •

Do something that enriches your life today. It doesn't have to be very special or important, provided it's something you enjoy and which makes you feel good about yourself. How about painting a picture if that's your idea of heaven, or relaxing with the Sunday papers if you've been slogging your guts out all week? It's a day for giving yourself a much-needed breather.

• *Monday 24 March* •

A certain person is fantastic company today. They're funny, clever and they really make you think. What's more, you'll rise to their level so it won't be long before you're equally sparkling company. A chance encounter could work out very well now, even if it doesn't seem that way at first. You might meet someone who does you a favour or who has some good advice for you.

• *Tuesday 25 March* •

There's a lot of tension in the air today and it isn't making you feel very comfortable. It seems that a certain person is on the warpath, especially if they feel that their reputation has been sullied in some way or you aren't taking them seriously enough. They appear to be ignoring the fact that they're doing a very good job of making a fool of themselves without any help from anyone else!

• *Wednesday 26 March* •

If you want to ask someone to do something, don't mention it today because it's highly likely that nothing will come of it. The person concerned might forget all about it or simply not want to do it but be unable to say so. Either way, you'll spend a lot of time and effort chasing them up or worrying whether everything will work out OK. Far better to wait until tomorrow before mentioning it.

• *Thursday 27 March* •

Anything exotic or unusual is right up your street during the coming month, so don't be afraid to experiment every now and then. You might decide to cook recipes that you've never tried before, or visit restaurants that you've avoided in the past because they seemed too weird for you. Another possibility is falling in love with someone who comes from a completely different walk of life, in which case it could happen much sooner than you think.

• *Friday 28 March* •

If you like the idea of falling for someone who's unusual or from a different background, keep your eyes peeled for them today. There's every chance that you might meet them, especially if this happens in ways you weren't expecting. For instance, you might bump into someone in the street and end up going out with them, or you may not hit it off at first even though you end up together. Wait and see!

• *Saturday 29 March* •

Someone's got a very sharp tongue today and it seems to be directed at you. What have you done to deserve this? Is it justified or are you the innocent party? Unfortunately, the atmosphere is so infectiously tense that you'll soon start to bite people's heads off as well. This won't help the situation because it will mean that you can't even ask someone if they'd like a cup of tea without running the risk of having a row.

• Sunday 30 March •

Thank heavens everyone has calmed down after yesterday's angst. It's your chance to make amends if needs be, or perhaps to turn the whole thing into a joke if you think that's a better approach. If you want to talk someone into seeing things from your point of view, do it today while your enthusiasm is at such a peak. How can anyone resist you when you're like this?

• Monday 31 March •

This is a fabulous day for getting on with plenty of work. You're able to go through things with a fine-tooth comb, especially if you're tackling red tape or official forms. It's also a good opportunity to get to the bottom of a difficult situation and to find out what's been going on. You'll soon know if someone isn't telling you the truth or is fudging the issue.

APRIL AT A GLANCE

Love	♥ ♥ ♥				
Money	£ $				
Career	💻	💻	💻	💻	💻
Health	☼ ☼				

• Tuesday 1 April •

Today's New Moon is asking you an important question: how are you progressing with your goals and ambitions? Are they within your grasp or do they seem as far away as ever? If you don't appear to be making much progress, or you're lacking confidence in yourself, use the coming fortnight as a chance to reawaken your interest and develop more faith in your abilities. You can do it!

• *Wednesday 2 April* •

You're not interested in generation gaps or anything else that divides you from other people today. Instead, you're keen to work on things that bring you together. For instance, if you're with someone who's much older than you, you'll enjoy talking to them and getting to know them as a fellow human being rather than feeling that you can't connect because you have nothing in common.

• *Thursday 3 April* •

Inject a little excitement into your world today. You aren't keen on jogging along as usual: you want to liven things up a little. A last-minute change of plan may take matters out of your hands and leave you scrabbling to catch up with what's going on, but even so you won't mind. You might also discover a fascinating book or TV programme that has you gripped.

• *Friday 4 April* •

Friends are wonderful company today and you'll really enjoy being with them. You might even be inspired to give one of them a treat, and if someone's birthday is coming up you'll do your utmost to buy them a super present or plan a lovely surprise for them. If you're lucky, someone will return the favour, even though that isn't why you're being so sweet.

• *Saturday 5 April* •

Between now and mid-June you'll enjoy thinking about your plans for the future and putting some of them into operation. These can vary from huge schemes that will take years to put into practice to minor plans that are just waiting for you to take the plunge. But rather than put things off any longer, why not promise yourself that you'll start at least one new project every week at the moment?

• *Sunday 6 April* •

The more interesting the company, the better the day you'll have. You're in the mood to chat to people who are avant-garde, unconventional or chalk to your cheese. Even if you sometimes find that a little of them goes a long way, you're quite happy to spend time with them now. If your thoughts stray to friends who live abroad, don't just think about them – get in touch with them and say hallo!

• *Monday 7 April* •

You're a huge support to someone today, and you may not even know it. You might listen to them when they're feeling down, or say something that makes them feel valued and appreciated. Encourage people to confide in you, provided you're willing to listen to them with an open mind and to respect their privacy. Alternatively, maybe you're the one who needs to talk things through.

• *Tuesday 8 April* •

Travel plans are really appealing today because you love the idea of taking off for pastures new. If you can't just drop everything and jump on a plane, plan your next trip so you've got something to look forward to. If a holiday is out of the question for the time being, why not consider going on a long weekend? If money is tight, maybe you could stay with friends or family? You'll love having a change of scene.

• *Wednesday 9 April* •

It's been an easy-going April so far but you hit trouble today. Someone is in a filthy temper and they don't care who they take it out on. You may not deserve a ticking-off but you'll get it all the same! Unfortunately, you may also start to feel frazzled after a while, especially if you're faced with a lot of work and not much time to do it in. If you need to let off steam, do it before things reach crisis point.

• *Thursday 10 April* •

This is a fabulous day to think carefully about your work and job satisfaction. Are you happy with the way things are going or does every day seem a complete waste of time? Even though you may be unable to wave a magic wand and change every-thing overnight, think about what you would like to alter and start considering how you're going to go about it. Don't be afraid to start small. Even huge oak trees were once tiny acorns!

• *Friday 11 April* •

If you're organizing a social event it won't be plain sailing today. Instead, you may have to cope with people who want everything arranged to suit them and who, quite frankly, don't seem to care about anyone else. There could also be a mini dust-up about how much everything is going to cost, so make sure everyone knows what's involved before you take things any further.

• *Saturday 12 April* •

Set aside time for your priorities in life today. Even if you have work to do, try not to devote the entire day to it unless it's the be-all and end-all of your existence. In your spare time, do something that makes you feel good about yourself and which gives you pleasure. You may also receive a pat on the back from someone whose opinion counts, making you feel like a million dollars.

• *Sunday 13 April* •

Oh dear. It seems that a certain person wants something for nothing today. Maybe they're expecting you to drop every-thing and cater to their every need, purely out of the goodness of your heart, or perhaps they're dropping some heavy hints and going into a sulk when you fail to come up with the goods. You wouldn't mind so much if they were going to reciprocate in some way, but it seems they want you to do all the giving while they do all the taking.

• *Monday 14 April* •

If you need some advice, listen carefully to what you're told today. It may not be entirely what you want to hear and you may dismiss some of it as being far too gloomy or cautious, but even so it contains nuggets of gold and you'd do well to notice them. If you're at work, you'll fare best if you can be left alone while you get on with whatever has to be done.

• *Tuesday 15 April* •

You'll thoroughly enjoy spending time and money on im-proving your home today. You might decide to make it more cosy or comfortable than it is at the moment, or you could be inspired to do great things in the garden. If you're feeling sociable, why not invite someone over to your place and entertain them in as lavish a style as possible? You're in the mood to cook some delicious food and break open a bottle.

• *Wednesday 16 April* •

You have one eye on the future at the moment and have been concentrating hard on your ambitions, but where does that leave your loved ones? You may not have noticed it until now, but perhaps they're feeling neglected or wondering where they fit into your new-found vision of life. It's important that you find a balance between the demands of your home and work now, even if it does take some juggling.

• *Thursday 17 April* •

Someone is all charm and no substance today. They have an ulterior motive, and if you're wise you'll try to fathom out what it is. Maybe it's a colleague who's doing their best to butter you up but who is leaving a saccharine taste in your mouth. Or it might be a friend who wants you to do something for them but hasn't got the guts to ask you outright. Try to get to the bottom of what's going on.

• *Friday 18 April* •

There's so much you want to do today that you don't know where to start. You'll also have very little patience with anyone who is holding you back or who doesn't have any sense of urgency. It won't be long before you're getting angry and possibly even giving this person a piece of your mind. However, don't throw your weight about unless you have a very good reason for it.

• *Saturday 19 April* •

You need a change of scene and a break in your routine today, otherwise you'll soon start to feel frazzled and drained. So do your best to give your usual Saturday schedule a miss and do something completely different instead. The more cooped up and bored you feel, the more likely it is that you'll become accident-prone or will say or do things that cause havoc.

• *Sunday 20 April* •

How is your social life looking at the moment? If you never seem to see your friends from one month's end to the next because there are always more pressing demands on your time, you need to do something about it during the coming four weeks. Set aside some time each week for being with chums, or join a group or club that will introduce you to some fresh faces.

• *Monday 21 April* •

Between now and mid-June you'll have a burning need to focus on activities and people that mean a lot to you. Anything or anyone that feels like a waste of time will get short shrift from you, even if you aren't aware of the message you're sending out. Your libido will also get a massive injection of energy, whether you express this sexually or channel it into other areas of your life.

• *Tuesday 22 April* •

Life is full of surprises today, and that's exactly the way you'll like it. Even if you're usually the sort of Cancerian who enjoys knowing what the day will bring, you'll feel stimulated by living from moment to moment right now. Go with the flow whenever possible because that will lead you into some interesting situations and introduce you to some fascinating people.

• *Wednesday 23 April* •

Take care today because you're feeling very vulnerable emotionally and could easily convince yourself that loved ones are being elusive or aren't very committed to you. As a result, you'll try to force them into reassuring you by showing their affection, even if they don't want to because they're busy with other things or they aren't in the mood. This will end up as a vicious circle, with you feeling unloved and needy, and partners feeling that they're being smothered. How can you resolve this?

• *Thursday 24 April* •

Find the time to tackle your official and joint finances today, especially if you're starting to worry about them or you're aware that you've been neglecting them recently. If you need to talk things over with someone first, do so now while you're in the mood. Ideally, you should avoid mixing friendship and money at the moment – they're uneasy bedfellows and could lead to bad feeling.

• *Friday 25 April* •

A certain person is a tower of strength today, making you very grateful to them. They're eager to help you in any way they can, even if that simply means listening while you tell them your troubles or letting you know that they care about what's happening to you. If you're involved in a charity or good cause, you'll want to work even harder than usual to help others now.

• *Saturday 26 April* •

This is a super day for being with friends and doing things that you enjoy. If you can spare the time, why not take off for the day and visit somewhere for the first time? You'll enjoy doing something that combines education and entertainment, such as going to a museum or art gallery. This is also a great chance to take part in a group activity that allows you to mix with others who are on the same wavelength as you.

• *Sunday 27 April* •

Try not to take on too much today. Otherwise you'll end up feeling like a piece of chewed string. Pace yourself, even if you've got the nagging sense that you'll never get everything done in time. You won't be much good to anyone if you end up ill and incapable of doing things. Watch out, too, for worries that eat away at you and assume monumental propor-tions. Are they really that serious?

• *Monday 28 April* •

Enjoy the rapport that exists between you and a certain person today, especially if you admire them for their expertise or wisdom. If you've been attracted to someone who's important or influential, what happens now will increase your hopes of getting a romantic relationship off the ground. Only time will tell, but in the meantime you can enjoy the warm glow of anticipation!

• *Tuesday 29 April* •

You're brimming with self-confidence today and it will propel you into all sorts of exciting areas. However, try not to bite off more than you can chew or make yourself out to be some sort of expert when you don't really know what you're doing! If you're buying items for a favourite hobby, you could quickly get carried away and get all sorts of things that you don't really need but can't resist.

• *Wednesday 30 April* •

Do someone a good turn today, even if you don't know them. You could drop some money into a collecting tin or buy an item from a charity shop. Or maybe you personally know someone who could do with a helping hand. You'll manage to do this in a supportive way without making them feel as though they're being a nuisance or you're playing Lord or Lady Bountiful.

MAY AT A GLANCE

Love	♥ ♥
Money	£ $ £
Career	💻 💻 💻
Health	☼ ☼

• *Thursday 1 May* •

If you've been having difficulties with a friend recently, how about giving them a second chance? During the coming fortnight, try to get to the bottom of what's gone wrong and do something about it. Today will also be a wonderful opportunity to expand your social life by joining a new club or organization that caters for one of your interests or will introduce you to people on the same wavelength as you.

• *Friday 2 May* •

Someone is tremendously helpful to you today and you're extremely grateful to them. It reminds you of how sweet and considerate some people can be. And before the day is out, a certain person may be saying that of you because it's highly likely that you'll also be doing someone a favour today. You may not even realize that you've done it, but you have.

• *Saturday 3 May* •

If there's one thing you enjoy today, it's spending money. It will give you enormous pleasure to buy items that are luxurious or will give you lots of happiness. You don't have to spend a small fortune, either, although you may be tempted to. If you pass someone holding a collecting tin for charity, you'll want to give generously.

• *Sunday 4 May* •

Take care because this looks like being a difficult day. You'll struggle to keep up your spirits, especially if you have to deal with someone who wants to make you feel bad. It will also be hard to deal with tough situations because your instincts will tell you to duck the issue and pretend it isn't happening. Yet that will only cause more problems than it solves, so try to face up to what's going on.

• *Monday 5 May* •

You're feeling rather withdrawn and silent today, making you want to keep yourself to yourself. It may even be a struggle to remain cheerful, thanks to lots of nagging doubts that are eating away at you and threatening your equilibrium. It will be horribly easy to allow problems and anxieties to get on top of you now, and also to imagine that these are worse than they really are.

• *Tuesday 6 May* •

The past two days have been rather grim but you're much more upbeat today, thank goodness. You may even be able to laugh at yourself and wonder why you've been so down in the mouth recently. Friends are especially good company now and will help you to dispel any remaining anxiety or depression. Immersing yourself in a favourite hobby is also good therapy now.

• *Wednesday 7 May* •

The people you work with have a very strong effect on you today. You may feel a powerful connection with one of them, perhaps transcending your working relationship and becoming something much more meaningful. It might lead to a strong friendship or it could be the start of a romantic or sexual relationship. This is also a marvellous day to put your heart and soul into what you're doing.

• *Thursday 8 May* •

Be careful if you're spending money today because it will flow through your fingers like water, given half the chance. You may not intend this to happen but, before you know it, you'll have bought all sorts of things. If you've been waiting for the opportunity to make a big play for someone wonderful, this is certainly a good day to do it but try not to go over the top unless you think that's your only option.

• *Friday 9 May* •

You have a strong need to establish your own identity today and to stop other people trying to own you or tell you what to do. This won't be easy, however, because they will probably feel threatened by your current need for independence and will therefore want to cling on tighter than ever. Of course it could work the other way round, with you being the one who's feeling tenacious and clingy. If so, watch out!

• *Saturday 10 May* •

You need plenty of variety in your life if you want to avoid things getting boring today. Even if you're usually a creature of habit, it will do you good to introduce some flexibility into your routine for a change. If you don't do this you'll find yourself on the receiving end of lots of disruptions that need patience and careful handling, both of which are in short supply at the moment.

• *Sunday 11 May* •

Get together with friends and close family today if you really want to enjoy yourself. It's a fantastic excuse to let your hair down in some convivial company. You'll also enjoy taking part in any sort of group activity, especially if it means you can mix with people who understand you or who share some of your enthusiasms.

• *Monday 12 May* •

Think twice before placing your trust in people today, particularly when it comes to your finances. Someone may have got their facts wrong and will therefore mislead you, or they might very deliberately pull the wool over your eyes. Even if you're making monetary decisions by yourself you might take the wrong option or get in a muddle. Your best bet is to leave well alone for the next few days, just to be on the safe side.

• *Tuesday 13 May* •

If you did make some financial decisions or listen to some-one's advice yesterday, the chances are that you're hopping mad today. Your reactions are a lot faster than usual and it won't take much to annoy you or put you on the defensive. This still isn't a good time to do anything of a financial nature because you might rush in where angels fear to tread, without thinking of the consequences.

• *Wednesday 14 May* •

Yet again, you should be wary of doing anything connected with your finances because the chances are that things will go pear-shaped. Instead, concentrate on your intimate relationships because they'll really benefit now from some close attention. You could get up quite a head of sexual steam with your other half, or maybe you'd prefer to connect on a different level. It will be quite a day!

• *Thursday 15 May* •

If you're angry with someone, it's important to say so today. Try to do this in as clear-cut and uncomplicated a manner as possible, without dredging up old scores that have nothing to do with the current situation. But be warned – if you're holding a grudge you'll be very tempted to make a real meal of it. Stick to the facts and don't allow yourself to get carried away by petty recriminations.

• *Friday 16 May* •

The coming fortnight is an excellent chance to clear the air with anyone who's annoyed you recently. This may mean that you have to eat humble pie or be the first to break the silence between you, but the results will be worth the slight loss of face that you suffer in the meantime. It might also be a poignant time in which you have to say goodbye to a loved one for some reason.

• *Saturday 17 May* •

Health concerns are uppermost in your mind today. You might be feeling slightly under the weather and be worrying about the causes. If so, don't be surprised if you end up imagining the worst because it's one of those days when your thoughts can get out of hand! You might also be concerned about a pet, in which case it's important to do whatever you can to help them.

• *Sunday 18 May* •

You crave interesting and stimulating company today, so try to mix with as many fascinating people as possible. Seek out anyone who makes you think or encourages you to view life from a different angle. You might also be powerfully attracted to someone you meet, even if they seem quite outrageous or aren't your usual type at all. For some strange reason, that makes them even more enticing at the moment.

• *Monday 19 May* •

Someone does their best to talk you into parting with your money today, but will they succeed? They're certainly giving it all they've got! Bear this in mind if you wander into a shop because you could be treated to the hard sell. If you're thinking of buying something for one of your hobbies or pastimes, don't be surprised if you decide to spend a lot more money than you intended. You won't be able to resist it!

• *Tuesday 20 May* •

You're in a fantastic mood today and you want it to last as long as possible. For that to happen, you need to do something sociable at some point. Get together with some friends, go out on the town or take your other half out for a meal. You'll have nothing to worry about if you're taking charge of a group activity because everyone will listen to you and you'll obviously be in command.

• *Wednesday 21 May* •

You start to retreat into your Cancerian shell from today, and you won't want to emerge fully until this time next month. This is the perfect excuse to have more time to yourself than usual, because you'll really value your own company and the chance to mull things over without any interruptions. You may also become interested in charity or voluntary work, or something else that involves being behind the scenes.

• *Thursday 22 May* •

Although you aren't feeling unfriendly, you don't want to be surrounded by people today. Ideally, you should spend time with some of your closest friends, talking about things that are dear to your heart or which you rarely discuss because they are so private or sensitive. This is a great chance to share your feelings with people who will respect your opinions and listen to what you have to say.

• *Friday 23 May* •

It's a difficult day, so mind how you go. You're in a peculiar mood because things that you've been trying to bury under the carpet are apparently determined to show themselves. So if you've been trying to turn a blind eye to a difficult situation, you'll be confronted by it now and forced into taking action over it. You may also feel offended when someone says things that you think are beyond the pale.

• *Saturday 24 May* •

None of us is as straightforward as we seem and we all have different aspects of our personalities that are waiting to be expressed. Today, you discover a new facet of your own personality and the more you try to push it one side, the more determined it will be to assert itself. Try to allow this unusual side of you to be revealed because it's saying something important about you and your current situation.

• *Sunday 25 May* •

You have tremendous will power and determination today, making you able to do almost anything you set your mind to. If this involves other people, do your best to win their co-operation before you start, rather than expecting them to fall into line simply because they feel bad about doing anything else. If you're at work you'll make fantastic progress and have good reason to feel pleased with yourself.

• *Monday 26 May* •

You're in the mood to have fun today! You'll grab any excuse to get together with friends and do something enjoyable, even if it's only very modest. This is also a good day for spending money but be warned that you could part with an awful lot of it and not even notice! Still, at least you'll have a good time, even if you do have to spend the coming month paying for it.

• *Tuesday 27 May* •

You have a wonderful way with words today, making you ultra-charming and affable. No wonder you're in such great demand right now! This is the perfect opportunity to get on the right side of people who you've fallen out with recently, or to ask someone a favour if you aren't sure of what the reception will be. Even if you get the brush-off, at least it will be delivered nicely.

• *Wednesday 28 May* •

Inject a little excitement into your day. It's exactly what you're in the mood for. Maybe you should give your usual Wednesday routine a miss and do something more interesting instead? Even going to a different café or sandwich bar for lunch will make the day seem brighter and more interesting. You could also hear about a topic that fires your imagination and makes you want to know more about it.

• *Thursday 29 May* •

It's a fabulous day for indulging yourself, especially if you invite some friends to come along and keep you company. Maybe you could all go out for a meal to one of your favourite restaurants, or at the very least nip into the pub for a quick drink after work. If you've recently met someone very fanciable and you want to know if they feel the same about you, you could get your answer today – and you'll be thrilled.

• *Friday 30 May* •

The more flexible you can be, the easier it will be to weather the interruptions that litter your day. For instance, if you're hoping for some peace and quiet you could be invaded by someone who won't stop talking. An event might be changed at the very last minute or a travel plan may have to be revised in the light of circumstances that are beyond your control. Do your best to go with the flow.

• *Saturday 31 May* •

The next couple of weeks are a fabulous chance to bring out aspects of your personality that have been hidden until now.

Is there something you've always wanted to do but have never had the guts to try? If so, why not do something about it now? If you're involved in a behind-the-scenes romance, your relationship is about to enter a very important new phase. Even if you aren't tied up in anything like that at the moment, you soon could be, so watch this space.

JUNE AT A GLANCE

Love	♥ ♥ ♥ ♥ ♥
Money	£ $ £
Career	💻 💻 💻 💻 💻
Health	☼ ☼ ☼ ☼ ☼

• *Sunday 1 June* •

You're in an assertive mood without wanting to go over the top and beat people around the head. It's an ideal day for getting across your point of view in a reasonable manner, so you stand a good chance of being heard. This is also an excellent day for sorting out any problems connected with your joint or official finances and encouraging other people to help you in any way they can.

• *Monday 2 June* •

Life offers some excitements today and you'll really enjoy them. Ideally, you should do something that departs from your usual schedule, especially if you feel slightly daring or naughty while you're doing it. If you're going near a bookshop, you could be very tempted to buy items that will give you plenty to think about or teach you something new about the world.

• *Tuesday 3 June* •

The more gullible and trusting you are, the more upsetting today will be. You should think twice before placing your faith in someone, particularly where money is concerned, because they might let you down either accidentally or deliberately. If you're offered the chance to sink some money into a get-rich-quick scheme, avoid it like the plague now because it's unlikely to bring you anything but disappointment, trouble or something even worse.

• *Wednesday 4 June* •

During the past couple of years you've sometimes been plagued by worries and anxieties that have lurked in the back of your mind, waiting to pounce on you when you're feeling vulnerable. That situation changes from today, thank goodness, making you much more determined to take constructive action about these worries. You will also give the impression of being more serious than usual at times.

• *Thursday 5 June* •

Even if you're usually very lovey-dovey with your other half, the battle lines are drawn between you today. Tensions connected with possessiveness or jealousy will cause endless problems and eventually lead to a row. Yet there will be something exciting and stimulating about this, so it's the perfect excuse to kiss and make up. It could be a very sexy experience!

• *Friday 6 June* •

There's no doubt that you've got your head screwed on the right way today. You're in a very sensible mood and are thinking along highly rational lines. If there's a lot you want to do today, you'll be most effective if you can plan ahead and therefore make the best use of your time. You may also be asked to give your opinion or advice about something, and you'll gladly do your best.

• Saturday 7 June •

Whoops! Someone could let the cat out of the bag today and drop you right in it. Or maybe you'll be the one who says the wrong thing? There's also the chance that you could become very irritated by what you see as someone's deliberate with-holding of information. You think they've been underhand and sneaky, and you don't care if they know it.

• Sunday 8 June •

Try to be easy on yourself today because you will have a tendency to take on too much responsibility or imagine that everyone's trying to get at you. You may also be worrying about a relative or loved one who isn't very well or who has other reasons for giving you cause for concern. It's one of those difficult days when things can quickly get on top of you unless you have some light relief.

• Monday 9 June •

If something is bugging you, the only answer is to take some constructive action now. You may be fretting about a health problem, such as some sinister symptoms, but the situation won't improve until you seek medical advice and find out exactly what's going on. If you've been promising yourself that you're going to take more care of your health, perhaps by giving up smoking, start right now.

• *Tuesday 10 June* •

Over the next few weeks it won't always be easy to express your feelings as freely as usual. You may feel constrained for some reason or you could be gripped by shyness, making you reluctant to wear your heart on your sleeve. Or maybe you don't want anyone to know how you feel because you're involved in a hush-hush relationship? Whatever your circumstances, you'll enjoy some wonderfully romantic moments.

• *Wednesday 11 June* •

If you're trying to get to the bottom of a financial conundrum, do something about it today while you're in the mood. You won't allow anyone to fob you off with lame excuses, and in fact they'll soon realize their mistake if they try because you simply won't stand for it. You could be a bit vociferous at times, which is great if that's what's needed but not so good if the other person doesn't deserve it.

• *Thursday 12 June* •

If you're currently trying to avoid someone, you can almost guarantee that you'll bump into them at some point today. It's one of those days when you can expect the unexpected, especially in your relationships. You may also be strongly attracted to someone who you usually can't stand or who would normally be a big turn-off. Yet, right now, you can't get enough of them. What is going on?

• *Friday 13 June* •

There will be times during the next couple of weeks when you feel you need to censor everything you say, or think twice before opening your mouth. This guardedness will protect you from putting both feet in it but may also make you seem slightly cagey or shifty at times. In fact, there may be occasions when you have to force yourself to say something because keeping silent won't be in your best interests.

• *Saturday 14 June* •

If you've decided to do something constructive about improving your health, today's Full Moon will give you further encouragement. You might even decide to do more than you first intended, such as combining giving up smoking with taking more exercise or drinking more water. During the coming fortnight you may also make an important decision about your current job situation.

• *Sunday 15 June* •

You're taking things rather seriously today and, as a result, could get into a bit of a panic about a relationship. If things aren't going very well with this person at the moment, it won't take much for you to convince yourself that your relationship is on the skids or that they've gone off you. However, you may be contributing to the situation by being rather off-hand or unfriendly. Try to cheer up.

• *Monday 16 June* •

If you ask someone to do something new today, don't be surprised if it all goes pear-shaped or comes to nothing. Equally, if someone offers to do you a favour now, it may turn out to be hot air. This isn't a good day to start anything new because it stands a very poor chance of being a success. Instead, use your time to check things that are already up and running, and to make sure they're going well.

• *Tuesday 17 June* •

You're gripped by a sense of adventure today that will make the next few months seem very exciting. You might decide to do something that you've never attempted before, simply to see if you can manage it. Travel plans may also grip you, filling you with dreams of visiting exotic destinations or somewhere that you've always wanted to visit. The more risks you're prepared to take, the more exciting life will be now.

• *Wednesday 18 June* •

You're in the mood to do some clearing out and tidying up today, so get cracking without delay. It will do you good to throw out things you no longer need, especially if you're the sort of Cancerian who usually hoards everything for far too long. While you're about it, check any equipment that you rely on to make sure it's working perfectly. If it isn't, either get it repaired or replace it now before it gives up the ghost just when you need it most.

• *Thursday 19 June* •

Love makes your world go round today and it isn't only romantic or sexual love, although they will both have a lot of meaning for you right now. You're eager to show loved ones how much they mean to you and to reassure them about the place they occupy in your heart. If there have been any rifts between you recently, this is a great chance to sort them out and get things back on an even keel.

• *Friday 20 June* •

You've got stars in your eyes today, thanks to the effect that a certain person is having on your heart. You're completely dazzled by them and probably can't think about much else.

It's a fabulous opportunity to bring out the born romantic inside you. How about going out for dinner together? Or maybe you'd prefer to stay at home and pretend that the rest of the world doesn't exist.

• Saturday 21 June •

You start to feel much more outgoing and confident from today, so enjoy it while it lasts over the coming month. Although there will still be occasions when you cherish some time to yourself, they won't be nearly as frequent and they'll be tempered by your need to get out there and make your mark on the world.

• Sunday 22 June •

What do you spend your money on? If you often ask yourself this question because you don't know where all your cash disappears to, this is an excellent day to think about it carefully. Once you do this you may realize that you don't buy big things but you buy lots of little things, or maybe it's the other way round. You will also be tempted to spend money today, especially on items that make you feel cosy.

• Monday 23 June •

Someone in your life needs to spread their wings and fly a little today. If it's you, it may feel rather strange, especially if you're the sort of Cancerian who is usually perfectly happy to stick to the familiar things in life. Suddenly, you want to spread your wings and explore new situations. If it's someone else who's feeling so independent, you may be threatened by their need for expansion and want to curb it. However, this will only make them even more determined to go their own way, much to your dismay.

• *Tuesday 24 June* •

Are you ready to make some exciting and radical changes to your life? Think about what you would like to alter about yourself and how you're going to go about it. Maybe there's something that you've always wanted to do but have never dared to try? Well, this is a fabulous opportunity to give it a go. After all, what have you got to lose? You may even discover that you enjoy putting yourself to the test and seeing if you've got what it takes.

• *Wednesday 25 June* •

You're full of dynamic energy today, especially when it comes to doing things that are exciting and challenging. Sheer adrenalin will carry you through the day and it will be highly addictive. If you've got the time you'll really enjoy getting out into the great outdoors, perhaps by going for a brisk walk. Ideally, you should get into the wide open spaces – you'll adore the feeling of freedom that comes over you.

• *Thursday 26 June* •

Things are unpredictable today, much to your disgust. You'll feel that you can't plan anything with any sort of confidence because you aren't sure how it's going to turn out. Existing arrangements may also require some juggling because someone changes their mind or moves the goalposts when you least expect it. Try to take life easy now or you'll end up as taut as an elastic band, and just as likely to snap.

• *Friday 27 June* •

If things got you down yesterday, your temper will now get the better of you. Trying to calm down will be almost impossible, especially if you fuel your irritation by running over all the things that have annoyed you so much. There could also be a difference of opinion about a travel arrangement or forthcoming holiday. Watch out, or you'll end the day fuming.

• *Saturday 28 June* •

Peace breaks out today after some rather turbulent recent encounters. Do your best to pour oil on troubled waters, especially if you have a nasty feeling that you've upset someone or over-reacted in the past few days. Once that's out of the way, you're free to relax. It's a wonderful day to visit somewhere beautiful or peaceful, such as a favourite stretch of countryside or a special church.

• *Sunday 29 June* •

Today's New Moon gives you a massive injection of energy and self-confidence that will carry you through the coming fortnight with distinction and promise. This is just what you need if you've been waiting for the right moment to get a new project off the ground or take the initiative in some way. Any ventures that were put on hold may also get the green light again any day now.

• *Monday 30 June* •

You have a very active mind today and it will lead you in some fascinating directions if you let it. However, it could be difficult keeping track of all the thoughts whizzing through your brain at the moment and at times you may get slightly disorientated. Write down all the clever ideas that come to you, in case you don't remember them later on.

JULY AT A GLANCE

Love	♥ ♥ ♥ ♥ ♥
Money	£ $ £ $ £
Career	💻 💻 💻 💻 💻
Health	☼ ☼ ☼ ☼ ☼

• *Tuesday 1 July* •

You're brimming with common sense today, making you the obvious person to turn to if someone is having a crisis or needs advice. However, your serious mood could soon make you sombre and rather inclined to be pessimistic. Beware of taking on more responsibility than usual and making a rod for your own back. You may also have doubts about your intellectual abilities.

• *Wednesday 2 July* •

You have a fabulous gift for putting your ideas into words today, especially if you want to enthuse someone or get them on your side. You'll soon manage to capture their interest. If you got bogged down yesterday, you're feeling much more positive today. You may even take a completely different view of problems that have beset you, seeing them as something to rise above rather than be swamped by.

• *Thursday 3 July* •

Whatever else you do today you'll want to spend some money at some point. It will give you infinite pleasure to treat yourself to something, even if it's only a bar of your favourite chocolate or a magazine. Of course, if you're feeling more adventurous than that and have the money to spare, you won't need any encouragement to splash out on some delicious indulgences.

• *Friday 4 July* •

You're blessed with infinite charm over the next few weeks and you'll be able to twist people round your little finger whenever you want to. This July will also work wonders for your ego because it's a great opportunity to spend some time and money on improving your appearance. Not that it needs improving, of course, but it never hurts to gild the lily! You might even fancy giving yourself a completely new look.

• *Saturday 5 July* •

You're very talkative today! You'll happily natter about whatever pops into your head, but try not to hog the conversation too much because other people may also have things that they want to talk about. It's also important to listen to what you're being told, rather than just wait for the other person to stop talking so you can carry on where you left off.

• *Sunday 6 July* •

There's no knowing who or what will attract you today, which is half the fun. You could be smitten by a new interest that completely grabs you or you might be thunderstruck by someone you meet, even if they aren't conventionally attractive. It's the unusual that fascinates you at the moment, so you won't be very keen on anyone or anything that's pedestrian, predictable or mundane.

• *Monday 7 July* •

Temper, temper! Someone's got steam coming out of their ears today and you'll want to put as much distance between you as possible. That may be difficult if it's a member of the family who's on the warpath. Are they making a big fuss about nothing or are they justified in being so angry? You may also be in a paddy about something, in which case try to deal with the facts rather than settle old scores.

• *Tuesday 8 July* •

Your emotions take a serious turn today. Is that because of something that's happened or are you mystified about why you're feeling a little blue? You're very sensitive to what's going on around you right now and are liable to read things the wrong way or interpret them in a very pessimistic fashion. For instance, you may tell yourself that you're a social disaster and that no one likes you, even though that isn't true. Come on, what's really wrong?

• *Wednesday 9 July* •

Thank goodness you're feeling so much better today! You're much more positive and cheerful, and you may even be wondering why you got into such a state yesterday. What's more, any fears that you had about a certain person may be put to rest because the atmosphere between you is so warm and loving. This is certainly a fabulous day for your love life, with you-know-who making you feel cherished. Aah!

• *Thursday 10 July* •

Are you doing too much? It certainly looks like it. You're dashing around like the White Rabbit from *Alice in Wonderland*, trying to do five things at once. Unfortunately, this means that you're unlikely to do anything properly because you're in such a flap, and it also means that you could end up being accident-prone and hurting yourself. Be very careful when handling anything hot or sharp, just in case.

• *Friday 11 July* •

You could fall in love today! But it won't necessarily be with a person; it might be with an idea or interest. For example, you could be bowled over by a book that you're reading, making you want to read more by that author or find out more on that subject. You might also feel pretty impassioned about a political or spiritual topic, perhaps wanting to get everyone around you interested in it as well.

• *Saturday 12 July* •

If you've had your doubts about a particular relationship recently, perhaps wondering whether it will continue for much longer, your worst fears could be realized today. You might decide that the cracks are continuing to grow between you or that you're drifting further apart from one another. Try not to do anything rash today: you may not be seeing things in their true light.

• *Sunday 13 July* •

Relationships come under the scrutiny of the Full Moon during the coming fortnight, encouraging you to reassess all your partnerships and decide whether they're working OK. Any difficulties are likely to come to a head between now and the end of the month, forcing you to do something about them. However, don't imagine that it's all or nothing because compromise may be the answer.

• *Monday 14 July* •

Are you ready to do some soul-searching? This is a marvellous day to examine your feelings with tremendous clarity and objectivity. You will even be able to admit to emotions that you aren't very proud of or which make you feel uncomfortable. However, this will take guts and you may be tempted to shy away from such thoughts. If you can stick with them, though, you'll learn a lot about yourself.

• *Tuesday 15 July* •

Trust your intuition today. It will send you some very important information about a close partner. You might get a strong impulse to talk to them about something specific, which turns out to be exactly the right thing to have done, or you may know that certain subjects mustn't be mentioned. You may even feel that there is no need for words because you're communicating so well on other levels.

• *Wednesday 16 July* •

Would you like a change of scene? If you haven't had a holiday yet this year, or you're feeling a bit bogged down with your usual routine, consider getting away this weekend or booking up a short trip in the next few weeks. It will do you a lot of good and you'll return feeling refreshed. It will be even better if you can visit somewhere for the first time.

• *Thursday 17 July* •

Give yourself a treat and surround yourself with beauty or culture today. You might decide to visit a local museum or art gallery. Or perhaps a trip to the cinema or theatre is more in your line? If you'd prefer to be outdoors, how about walking in a favourite park or stretch of countryside, or even having a picnic in the garden?

• *Friday 18 July* •

Optimism really pays off today, so keep cheerful. You could be offered a marvellous opportunity, or you might decide to

make the best of a difficult situation and turn it into something positive. Anything connected with education, travel,
spirituality, ecology or history is right up your street now and
you'll really enjoy immersing yourself in it.

• *Saturday 19 July* •

Keep a close eye on your belongings today and try not to let
them out of your sight. There's a possibility that a light-
fingered so-and-so might take a fancy to one of your possessions and decide to filch it. You should also be careful when
buying or selling anything, in case you're short-changed or
involved in something that turns out to be dishonest. Even if
someone isn't deliberately trying to rook you, they may get
their sums wrong or accidentally give you false information.

• *Sunday 20 July* •

This is a wonderful day for being with older friends and
relatives. You'll really appreciate their company and will want
to say so. You could get quite sentimental, especially if you
encourage them to talk about their past. It's also a good
opportunity to improve your relationship with a boss or
superior by making an effort to draw them out and get them
talking about themselves. They'll revel in it!

• *Monday 21 July* •

Things were going swimmingly with older people yesterday
but something seems to have gone wrong overnight. Perhaps
you misunderstand one another, the generation gap gets in
the way or an ancient resentment rears its ugly head. One way
to deal with this is to channel all your angst and irritation into
your work. You could end up achieving a lot more than you
expect.

• Tuesday 22 July •

You're in a very exacting and precise mood, making it a fantastic day for going over details and checking facts. For instance, if you've been meaning to check your bank or credit card statements, this is the perfect opportunity to tackle them. You'll soon spot any mistakes that have been made. If you've been worried about a strange symptom or ailment, it makes sense to talk to a medical expert now.

• Wednesday 23 July •

Your priorities are highlighted during the next four weeks and you could be surprised at what you discover about yourself. You might decide, for example, that your material needs aren't nearly as important as you thought and that you're currently more concerned about your family or your relationships. Even so, it will be second nature for you to put a value on everything and everyone you encounter, which may not always be helpful.

• Thursday 24 July •

Give yourself a treat today and concentrate on things and people that mean a lot to you. You won't want to make a big song and dance about this, and will prefer to keep your feelings as private as possible. A good cause or charity will also attract your attention, and if you decide to donate something to it you'll want to give as much as you can. This could be money or it might be your time.

• Friday 25 July •

Someone tells you a secret today, but first they'll want to know that you won't blab their personal business to all and sundry. You won't, of course, but you may have to convince them of that fact. Whatever they tell you will be precious and you should take it as a compliment that they want to confide in you.

• *Saturday 26 July* •

If you're currently making plans about something, you'll be highly optimistic about the financial side of it today. You may even persuade yourself that it will cost much less than you thought, or that you can afford to spend a lot more money than you originally decided. However, before you get too excited, remind yourself that you may be overlooking some salient facts or even trying to kid yourself. Be careful!

• *Sunday 27 July* •

The more active you are today the better you'll feel. You don't want to get stale or bogged down from not having enough mental or physical stimulation. Even if you can't be physically active for some reason, that doesn't mean you have to let your brain stultify. Get involved in a project or venture that fills you with excitement, or talk to someone who always captures your imagination.

• *Monday 28 July* •

You're very interested in your appearance at the moment, and this is the perfect day to make yourself look even more attractive than usual. You might decide to go to the hairdresser or maybe you fancy buying yourself some new clothes. If you need to do something less expensive, even buying some modest accessories will help to brighten up your existing outfits and make you feel more stylish.

• *Tuesday 29 July* •

The astrological accent is shining on your values and priorities at the moment, and during the coming fortnight you'll bene-fit from thinking about them in a lot of detail. If you suspect that your life is unbalanced, with too much emphasis on one side of it and not enough on another, this is an excellent time to start doing something about it.

• *Wednesday 30 July* •

Pay extra attention to the way you communicate during the next couple of months. This will be your key to getting on well with the people around you. If you often feel tongue-tied around a certain person, make an effort to get to know them better now. It will also be a good idea to improve the means by which you communicate with others, such as upgrading your mobile phone or buying a new gadget for your computer.

• *Thursday 31 July* •

A certain someone is being incredibly contrary today. If you say something is black, they'll tell you it's white. It's enough to drive you round the bend. But before you puff up with right-eous indignation, consider that people may find you rather irritating at the moment too. Perhaps you're being equally pernickety and stubborn, yet stoutly refusing to admit to it. Having a change of scene or breaking your usual Thursday routine may help you to snap out of it.

AUGUST AT A GLANCE

Love	♥ ♥ ♥ ♥
Money	£ $ £ $ £
Career	💻 💻
Health	☼ ☼ ☼

• *Friday 1 August* •

It's awfully easy for people to get things out of proportion today. They might make a big song and dance about something that they'd usually shrug off, or they may examine something in excruciating and compulsive detail. You may also find it hard to keep things in proportion, especially where your work and health are concerned. Keeping active and busy will help to counter this.

• *Saturday 2 August* •

What's up? You aren't feeling very cheerful today. Perhaps you're worried about a loved one's welfare or are concerned about a domestic problem. However, it's just as likely that you can't put your finger on what's wrong and so feel wretched without knowing why. You need an antidote to all this, otherwise you'll just make yourself more miserable as the day goes on.

• *Sunday 3 August* •

You're feeling much better today and more able to face up to any problems that are besetting you at the moment. It's a super day for taking care of your house, perhaps by being creative in the garden or doing some decorating indoors. Even picking some flowers for the house or altering the décor slightly will make a big difference to the feel of the place, and to your mood.

• *Monday 4 August* •

Confusion reigns today, so take care. You might be in a quandary about a financial matter, in which case your best option is to sit tight until things get clearer. Or you may be in two minds about an emotional problem, not knowing which way to turn. Be very honest with yourself about your motives and try to be as straightforward with others as possible. Fudge issues and they'll come back to haunt you.

• *Tuesday 5 August* •

After yesterday's indecision, you're feeling much more sure of yourself. If you need to reach a decision you'll weigh up the facts first and take action only when you're sure you know what you're doing. This is also a good opportunity to review any decisions you made at the start of July. If you feel you made the wrong choice, now is the time to try to make amends.

• *Wednesday 6 August* •

If you're angry about something at the moment, it will be very difficult to control yourself today. You may end up yelling at someone or giving them a piece of your mind, delivered in no uncertain terms. Although it's important for you to clear the air if something is bothering you, try not to do it in such a way that your behaviour makes the situation worse than it already is. In other words, don't be rude!

• *Thursday 7 August* •

You're easily seduced today! You could be tempted into spending lots of money on things that take your fancy, or you might be bewitched by someone who is very attractive and who you can't resist. If you're involved in any form of finance today, make sure you know what's going on in case someone is trying to fleece you or take advantage of your good nature.

• *Friday 8 August* •

Try to get together with someone unusual or interesting today. You aren't very keen on anyone who is a stick-in-the-mud or who clings to the past like a limpet, even if you normally have a lot of sympathy with them. Instead, you're in a forward-thinking mood and want to seem as progressive as possible. You may also surprise yourself by being receptive to many more ideas than usual.

• *Saturday 9 August* •

Make the most of your dynamic energy today, especially when it comes to accepting challenges or pushing yourself further than usual. If you want to persuade someone to see things from your point of view, this is definitely the day to do it because your enthusiasm is so catching. It's also a great day for visiting somewhere that you've never been to before or getting to know someone new.

• *Sunday 10 August* •

If you want to make some changes in your life, this is the perfect opportunity to spring into action. Maybe you need to make some alterations to the way you structure your finances, such as changing bank accounts or putting your savings into a more remunerative scheme? If so, do the background work on it today. You might also make some important decisions about your current job or a health problem.

• *Monday 11 August* •

Be wary when handling important or official money matters today because things could easily go slightly haywire. You might get the wrong end of the stick or be given misleading information, or you may simply be trying to turn a blind eye to something unpleasant or difficult that you don't want to think about. If in doubt, take action from tomorrow, when things are clearer.

• *Tuesday 12 August* •

Today's Full Moon picks up on the theme of your finances and, over the next two weeks, it will make the situation a lot clearer than it's been lately. Any indecision that you've been experiencing will be remedied and replaced with a greater clarity of vision. You may also find that certain situations sort themselves out, making it much easier to know how to handle them. What a relief!

• *Wednesday 13 August* •

Make the most of your powers of concentration today because they're ace! You'll be able to focus on things without fear of distraction, although that won't be the case if you spend the entire day on one activity without having a break from it. Not even you are superhuman! If you're taking some sort of test or exam today, you'll have nothing to fear and may not even have as many pre-test nerves as usual. Phew!

• *Thursday 14 August* •

More haste, less speed! You're trying to do everything at twice your normal pace today but unfortunately that could soon lead to you getting flustered and agitated. Much to your irritation, you could also become all fingers and thumbs so you end up taking more time than usual to do things. Try to slow down, take a deep breath and take things more easily.

• *Friday 15 August* •

You need to be in the limelight in some way today. This might mean getting a pat on the back from your boss or superior, or being fêted by someone else. You certainly need recognition for all your recent efforts and will feel remarkably hard-done-by if you don't get it. Things may also get on top of you more than normal, so you could have an emotional outburst at some point.

• Saturday 16 August •

You have a strong sense of responsibility today but it could weigh rather heavily on your shoulders after a while. For instance, you may take on more work than you can reasonably handle, or agree to do something out of a sense of duty, even though you don't know how you're going to fit it in with everything else that is going on. Try not to saddle yourself with more than you can comfortably manage.

• Sunday 17 August •

People are easy to get along with today, especially if they happen to be older, wiser or more influential than you. This will be a great relief, especially if you've got to see someone who isn't always the most comfortable companion. It's also a good day to think about your values and priorities in life, particularly in relation to your career and long-term goals. Is everything in balance or is something skew-whiff?

• Monday 18 August •

How do you feel about spending some money today? You probably don't need any encouragement to put your hand in your pocket right now. Besides, you're in the mood to treat yourself to something nice, such as a new outfit or some jewellery. You'll enjoy buying items that make you look and feel good, especially if they're made from natural materials or have a wonderful texture.

• *Tuesday 19 August* •

You're feeling very communicative today and will really enjoy chatting to whoever happens to be around. You don't really mind what you talk about just now – what's important to you is to make contact with others. It's a super day to get together with friends and catch up on all the gossip, or you might decide to have a blitz on your e-mails and write all those replies that you've been meaning to get round to.

• *Wednesday 20 August* •

Money and friends don't mix today. In fact, they're likely to curdle and leave a nasty taste in your mouth. Someone's nose might be put out of joint because they feel envious of another person's possessions or apparent good fortune, so it isn't a good idea to talk about your belongings or draw attention to them in any way. If you find yourself feeling jealous of someone, ask yourself why this should be.

• *Thursday 21 August* •

Once again, money burns a big hole in your pocket today, but what a good time you'll have in the process! It will give you enormous pleasure to browse in your favourite shops or to leaf through a mail order catalogue and decide to treat yourself to something. If you're involved in a celebration, you'll want to make it as enjoyable and special as possible.

• *Friday 22 August* •

Between now and the middle of September will be a fabulous time for getting out and about. If you want to increase your social circle, you couldn't have picked a better time to do it. People will respond very favourably to you, so it's also a great opportunity to break the ice with someone and get to know

them better. You might even fall for someone who lives locally
– maybe even on your doorstep.

• *Saturday 23 August* •

You're fascinated by what makes people tick today and the
more interesting their characters, the more intrigued you'll be.
You might even go out of your way to talk to someone who's
unusual or eccentric, but who is sometimes a bit too much for
you. Not today, however! If you get involved in a conversation
about a controversial subject, don't be surprised if the atmosphere becomes rather heated.

• *Sunday 24 August* •

You have a powerful urge to buck trends and break rules this
weekend. The more constrained and hidebound you feel, the
more you'll want to break out and do something drastic. Try to
let off steam in positive and constructive ways sooner rather
than later; otherwise you really will cause havoc by doing
things that raise eyebrows or by saying something that you'll
regret when you've calmed down.

• *Monday 25 August* •

Whatever else you do, try to do something that means a lot to
you today. If you don't, you'll feel that you're missing out
somehow and will end up rather dissatisfied. So get together
with someone who makes your world go round, relax in some
peaceful surroundings if that's what you crave, or devote some
time to a favourite hobby.

• *Tuesday 26 August* •

A special person easily gets hot under the collar today, so you
can expect some fireworks. The more emotionally involved

you are with them, the more likely you are to fall out with them. One of the best ways to deal with this is to avoid letting it get personal, and to try to retain your sense of humour. Look on it as a chance to clear the air and then enjoy kissing and making up afterwards.

• *Wednesday 27 August* •

Your communication skills get a huge boost from today, and you'll enjoy this for the next year. It will be a terrific opportunity to make some new contacts, some of whom could become friends. Day-to-day connections could turn out to be lucky, perhaps because someone makes some helpful suggestions or points you in directions you would never have found off your own bat. So keep talking!

• *Thursday 28 August* •

Adrenalin surges through you today, making you feel dynamic and energetic. The last thing you want to do is to sit around twiddling your thumbs, especially if you have something more exciting on the agenda. All the same, try to avoid throwing yourself into situations head first without thinking them through first. Although you want to get going, you don't want to do anything rash or foolish.

• *Friday 29 August* •

You're feeling very chatty and talkative today. Don't be surprised if you run up a big phone bill now! If you can't afford to chat on the phone for long, write lots of letters or send some e-mails. Something to watch out for is a slight tendency to blurt things out or say things in the heat of the moment and, once you've calmed down, to wonder what on earth possessed you.

• *Saturday 30 August* •

Are you ready to introduce some big changes into your life? Let's hope so because the stage is set for them at the moment. You might be ready to make some big decisions about someone's education, or maybe you're considering embarking on a massive journey or a once-in-a-lifetime holiday. Grab any experience that will broaden your horizons and give you a greater understanding of the world around you.

• *Sunday 31 August* •

You're bouncing around, full of beans today. You might decide to do something that's quite adventurous or daredevil, although you won't want to go over the top. If you're at home at the moment and don't have anything exciting planned, how about taking off on the spur of the moment and visiting somewhere for the first time, or doing something that gets the adrenalin pumping through your veins?

SEPTEMBER AT A GLANCE

Love	♥ ♥ ♥
Money	£ $
Career	💻 💻
Health	☼ ☼ ☼

• *Monday 1 September* •

Enjoy your social life today because it's full of promise. It's a fabulous day for getting together with some of your favourite people, even if you don't do anything very exciting. Even a quick drink after work, a trip to the cinema or a cup of coffee at lunchtime will help to set you up for the week ahead. A loved one will say or do something that makes you feel fantastic.

• *Tuesday 2 September* •

You're sociable and good-humoured today. You also have the knack of appealing to other people's better natures, so it's almost guaranteed that they'll behave well towards you. Make the most of your ability to express yourself now. You might do that by writing in your diary, making up a fairy story for the children or putting pen to paper in other ways.

• *Wednesday 3 September* •

You're blessed with a lot of common sense today, so put it to good use. If someone is trying to come up with ideas or solve a problem, you'll have some good contributions to make to the conversation. You certainly have your feet on the ground at the moment. You won't be interested in anything that's avant-garde or radical because you're keener right now on following tradition.

• *Thursday 4 September* •

You're very drawn to the unusual today, both where people and places are concerned. You might decide to break out of your normal Thursday routine, which will certainly do you a lot of good. It will also help you to gain more objectivity if you're currently battling with a difficulty or worry that doesn't want to go away. After you've had a break it won't seem nearly so oppressive.

• *Friday 5 September* •

A certain person is a very tricky customer today and they need careful handling. They're using a lot of emotional blackmail in an attempt to get their own way, although whether they succeed is another matter. If you try to stand up to them, you'll be in for quite a fight. That doesn't mean you should allow them to ride roughshod over you, but it does mean you should take responsibility for your behaviour and try not to get out of control. Let them do that, but not you.

• *Saturday 6 September* •

In most relationships there are tiny niggles and problems that come back to haunt you every now and then. This is a super day for doing your best to talk them through and, preferably, put them behind you. You might even manage to share a joke about some of your old differences. You're in a very understanding and conciliatory mood right now, so put it to good use.

• *Sunday 7 September* •

Whatever you're doing today, you'll want to give it your best shot. If you usually hold yourself back, you'll want to give much more right now. But if you normally go the whole hog anyway, you could easily over-reach yourself now and not know when to stop. Yes, you're in the mood for a challenge but don't be foolhardy.

• *Monday 8 September* •

You're such a diplomat today! You have an uncanny ability to say the right thing at the right time, even if this isn't usually your forte. Enjoy it while it lasts! It's just what you need if you've got to talk to someone you see on a regular basis but who isn't exactly the easiest person in the world, such as a cantankerous neighbour or a curmudgeonly relative. They will seem almost human at the moment!

• *Tuesday 9 September* •

Fancy a challenge? You want something to get your teeth into today; something that you feel is worthy of your talents and abilities. You'll enjoy seeing what you're capable of, but try not to go overboard or set yourself a goal that's over-ambitious and which you'll soon get tired of. It will be a lot more satisfying in the long run to do something that you know is within your grasp but which is still difficult, than to attempt to achieve the impossible and fail.

• *Wednesday 10 September* •

Life isn't nearly as black and white as you might imagine during the coming fortnight. You'll have to wrestle with problems that aren't easily solved or which mean you have to see situations from more than one viewpoint. You may also have to revise your view about a moral or philosophical question which always seemed quite straightforward in the past. Suddenly you're not so sure.

• *Thursday 11 September* •

It's a super day for keeping in touch with people. You're in a chatty mood and if you have to spend too long by yourself you'll start to feel as though you're going to burst. It's definitely a day for keeping on the move and having as much contact with others as possible. Any local event or neighbourhood gathering will be especially good now and you may also be intrigued by some gossip that you're told.

• *Friday 12 September* •

You feel a bit like a workhorse today, and also as though you'll never get through all the tasks that are waiting for you. Rather than wear yourself out by taking on too much, arrange to do things in their order of priority. After all, you can only do your best and anyone who expects more than that from you is living in cloud cuckoo land.

• *Saturday 13 September* •

If you felt overwhelmed by work yesterday, try to think things through today. Maybe it would help to talk to a superior or colleague, and to explain how you feel. This is also a good day to revise your daily schedule in some way, perhaps making more time for yourself or enabling you to fit in all your commitments as well as maintain your private life.

• *Sunday 14 September* •

You're full of bounce and energy today, and it feels great! Ideally, you should do something that's a complete departure from your usual Sunday schedule. You also fancy getting involved in some sort of adventure. How about having a day trip to a nearby town or doing something slightly daring, which reminds you that you're alive?

• *Monday 15 September* •

During the coming four weeks you'll get a big kick out of lavishing time, energy and possibly money on your home and family. You might decide that a domestic facelift is long overdue, and that it's time to redecorate your home or give it some artistic flourishes. You're not just interested in doing functional things now: you want to express your artistic streak in lots of different ways.

• *Tuesday 16 September* •

Concentrate on your social life whenever you get the chance today. You'll really enjoy being with friends or anyone else who happens to be on the same wavelength as you. For instance, if you've decided that you want to get to know some new people, this is a terrific opportunity to join a club, organization or anything else that will introduce you to some fresh faces.

• *Wednesday 17 September* •

As a Cancerian you need some time to yourself every now and then, and this is definitely one of those occasions. It's not that you're feeling antisocial, it's simply that you'll relish being left alone for a while so you can do whatever you want, even if it's just staring at the wall. Once you've done that, you'll be able to join in with whatever is going on around you with more enthusiasm.

• *Thursday 18 September* •

It's another day when you crave your own company, but the feeling is stronger than it was yesterday. You may also have a very low tolerance threshold today, making you extremely impatient with anyone who's foolish, boneheaded or has other ways of annoying you. As if that weren't enough, you may also have to cope with a secret that's suddenly revealed, causing red faces all round.

• *Friday 19 September* •

This is a fantastic day for gathering as many of your nearest and dearest around you as possible. You're feeling slightly sentimental and nostalgic, so will adore the idea of having all your loved ones with you. It's also a great day for making some home improvements, whether you're starting a big project or simply doing some tidying up. You'll enjoy buying items that make your home more attractive or cosy.

• *Saturday 20 September* •

There have been times over the past couple of weeks when communications haven't been as easy or smooth as usual, but thankfully things start to get back to normal from today. If you've sent someone a letter or e-mail and have yet to receive a reply, it might be a good idea to chase them up to make sure they received it in the first place. It might have got lost in transit.

• Sunday 21 September •

The more active and busy you are today, the happier you'll feel. You'll love keeping on the move, especially if that means making contact with lots of different people and really feeling that you're in the swing of things. Get chatting to some of your neighbours, especially if you want to oil the wheels between you and a certain someone.

• Monday 22 September •

How are your domestic improvements coming along? You fancy spending some money on them today, whether that means raiding one of your favourite shops for furnishings or ornaments, or buying something by mail order or through the Internet. The whole process of choosing what to buy and finding the right items will be half the pleasure, so luxuriate in it.

• Tuesday 23 September •

Between now and this time next month you'll really enjoy being among familiar faces and places. You're still feeling the pull of adventure and new surroundings, but you'll want to balance these with the joy of being at home and with loved ones. You might want to make more of a fuss of your nearest and dearest than normal, but make sure you allow them to go their own way as well.

• Wednesday 24 September •

If you're involved in some form of financial arrangement with a loved one, you'll want it to run as smoothly as possible right now. That may mean that you're willing to allow any little niggles to pass you by, and to be as accommodating and understanding as possible. However, there's a chance that it may also mean you are prepared to turn a blind eye to any current problems and to hope they'll go away of their own accord. But will they?

• *Thursday 25 September* •

Look after yourself today because your emotions are slightly raw and you could easily be hurt by others. If someone isn't very chummy or doesn't have time to see you, you'll immediately assume the worst and will soon make yourself very miserable about it. Try to deal with the facts rather than allow your fears to get out of hand.

• *Friday 26 September* •

Today's New Moon is giving you the green light about all the domestic improvements you're currently involved in. If you've been waiting for the go-ahead on a project, you could soon be hearing some good news. If you've been toying with the idea of moving house but haven't taken it very seriously, you may become gripped with excitement about it and want to set the ball rolling as soon as possible.

• *Saturday 27 September* •

You see a new side to a well-loved person today. They may reveal episodes from their past that you knew nothing about, or they might do something that makes you view them in a completely fresh light. If you share a bank account or have some other form of financial arrangement with someone, this is a good opportunity to check that it's working OK and, if not, to do something about it.

• Sunday 28 September •

If you're unsure about anything or anyone, you'll want to examine it from all sides today. You're in the mood to pull things apart and see how they work, whether literally or metaphorically. This is fantastic if you're trying to get to the bottom of a mystery because you won't rest until you've got the answers. However, don't allow yourself to become like a grand inquisitor, demanding the truth about things that are none of your business or relentlessly questioning someone.

• Monday 29 September •

Think about your relationships today, especially those with your family and colleagues. If you're horribly aware of tension between you and a certain person, start considering how you can ease the pressure. Maybe talking to them will do the trick, or perhaps you need to come up with some clever ideas on your own. This is also a good day for making your working surroundings more relaxing or attractive.

• Tuesday 30 September •

You're in an organized mood today and will get satisfaction from checking that everything is running smoothly, both at home and at work. For instance, check the kitchen cupboards to make sure you haven't run out of any essentials and also that you've got all the personal items you need. At work, make sure your equipment is functioning properly.

OCTOBER AT A GLANCE

Love	♥ ♥ ♥ ♥ ♥
Money	£ $
Career	💻 💻
Health	☼ ☼ ☼

• *Wednesday 1 October* •

You're caught in the grip of some very strong emotions today and at times they may almost overwhelm you. It will be hard to maintain a sense of perspective and you could get swept up in whatever happens to be bugging you at the moment. If you're at work, you could get het up about a job or a colleague. You may also be grappling with worries about your health, in which case you need to talk to an expert.

• *Thursday 2 October* •

It's another day when your feelings are very close to the surface. Even if you think you're hiding them really well, they will be very apparent to everyone around you, so be warned! You may also feel rather defensive and therefore behave as though people are out to get you, even if they aren't. Try to keep cool, otherwise you'll end the day feeling like a piece of chewed string.

• *Friday 3 October* •

It hasn't been a very good start to October, because today you're feeling vulnerable and defenceless. At this point you should ask yourself what's going on. Is something worrying you or has something nasty happened, making you feel at sixes and sevens? Things will soon improve but in the meantime you need to get to the bottom of why you're so easily rattled.

• Saturday 4 October •

You're feeling a lot calmer today, thank goodness, and long may it last! Celebrate by doing something that you always enjoy or which feels like complete luxury. It's also a wonderful day for being with some of your nearest and dearest, especially if they pamper you in some way. Right now, you can do with all the tender loving care you can get! What's more, you're happy to dish it out yourself.

• Sunday 5 October •

You're still happy to be surrounded by dear and familiar faces, especially if you're on home turf or territory that you know very well. Today is a good opportunity to sort out the finances connected with a domestic arrangement or your current home improvement plans. If you're involved in a property deal at the moment, check your sums to make sure you can afford everything you're planning.

• Monday 6 October •

Your sense of duty is very strong today and, if you aren't careful, it could become overdeveloped. As a result you may take on tasks that aren't really your responsibility, purely because you want to give a good impression or because your conscience pricks you. Listen to the way you're talking to yourself. Are you telling yourself that nothing you're doing is quite good enough at the moment?

• Tuesday 7 October •

During the next two weeks your thoughts will automatically gravitate towards the past whenever they get the chance. You'll enjoy mulling over old times, in true Cancerian style. It will be even better if you can share memories with someone who experienced the original events with you. It will be enjoyable to reminisce but try to remember you're living in the present, not the past.

• *Wednesday 8 October* •

Think twice before embarking on any official or bureaucratic projects today. Anything with the slightest whiff of red tape is likely to fall at the first fence if you try to get it under way now. It might even end up being a lot more trouble than it's worth or landing you in hot water. Instead, concentrate on ventures that have already begun.

• *Thursday 9 October* •

Whenever you get the chance, try to dedicate the rest of October to love, laughter and enjoyment. Even if life is very difficult at the moment and you can't see much to smile about, it will do you good to have lots of breathers from your problems and to relax every now and then. If life is already very sweet, it could get a whole lot sweeter this month, especially where some of your favourite people are concerned. You might even start a love affair, or fall for your current partner all over again.

• *Friday 10 October* •

You're very wrapped up in your home and family at the moment. Does that mean you're neglecting your career or letting your ambitions idle on the sidelines? If so, you'll have to redress the balance during the coming fortnight. It will be better to do this yourself before you get ticked off by a superior or authority figure for not pulling your weight.

• *Saturday 11 October* •

This is a fantastic day for mending things. That might mean repairing a relationship that's hit a sticky patch, and doing your best to restore it to some sort of working order. Or it might mean physically repairing an appliance or object that's gone wrong or got broken, so you can use it again. Even if something hasn't ground to a halt just yet but looks as though it might, pay it some attention now. A stitch in time . . .

• *Sunday 12 October* •

You're conscientious today and want to do as good a job as possible, whatever you tackle. You'll also happily help a friend if they need some assistance, and won't rest until you know you've done what you can. If you're involved in an altruistic or humanitarian project or campaign at the moment, this is a great day to check that it's running smoothly or put in a few hours' work on it.

• *Monday 13 October* •

Give someone the benefit of the doubt today. You may have had your suspicions about them and you might even be perfectly well aware that they haven't behaved very well lately, but even so you're now ready to let bygones be bygones. This says a great deal about your understanding and compassion. Yet you are also aware that you would like others to forgive you when you transgress, and want to do the same in return.

• *Tuesday 14 October* •

Look out today because worries are threatening to get on top of you. Something is eating away at you, making you feel anxious and upset. To make matters worse, you may feel unable to confide in anyone, perhaps because you've convinced yourself that you're in the wrong. Try not to be so hard on yourself if it isn't truly warranted, and remember you may be rather pessimistic at the moment.

• Wednesday 15 October •

After yesterday's difficult moments, you deserve something nice to happen today and it does. It won't have to be very important to make you feel better. A loved one might give you a massive hug or tell you how much they care about you, or you may simply realize that you were taking everything far too seriously yesterday. If you're doing some tidying up you could find something that you'd completely forgotten about.

• Thursday 16 October •

You crave some excitement today, so what do you have in mind? Travel plans are especially enticing right now and if you haven't had a holiday this year you'll be champing at the bit by now. Maybe this is the day to book something? If your Christmas plans are still up in the air, you might be tempted to arrange a December holiday. It feels as though anything is possible.

• Friday 17 October •

This is a fantastic day for setting your mind at rest about anything that's worrying you. For example, if you're anxious about a health matter, this is the day to speak to an expert and find out what's going on. Equally, if you're bothered about a relative or child and want to find out what's happening, this is the day to talk to them. Ask them gently what's wrong; don't go in with all guns blazing!

• Saturday 18 October •

Enjoyment is top of your list of priorities today and you'll want to devote as much time to it as possible. So how do you plan on doing that? If you're going to a party or some sort of celebration, you'll want to have as much fun as you can get.

You might draw the line at tap dancing on the tables or wearing a lampshade for a hat, but that won't stop you being the life and soul of the proceedings.

• Sunday 19 October •

Things are not what they seem today. That should come as a relief, because you're feeling besieged and uncomfortable. You're also worried about things that you almost dare not put a name to because they have such power to upset you at the moment. Do your utmost to keep a firm grip on reality now and remind yourself that your imagination may be running away with you.

• Monday 20 October •

Grab the chance to boost your relationship with a certain person today. You'll enjoy establishing a strong rapport with them. Even if you're already in one another's pockets, you'll get a huge kick out of forging an even stronger link with them now. If you're talking to a child, you'll want to remind them that you love them while encouraging them to stand on their own two feet.

• Tuesday 21 October •

You'll enjoy spending money on your home today. You don't have to part with a fortune either, although you may be tempted! Even if you're doing some mundane shopping, such as getting the weekly groceries in your local supermarket, you'll soon get carried away and want to buy lots of edible goodies for your loved ones. These will be hard to resist.

• Wednesday 22 October •

Most Cancerians enjoy holding on tightly to the past and to their loved ones, but you're prepared to lessen your grip today.

This is good because it will allow you to enjoy what's going on around you without feeling the need to compare it with previous experiences. You may even want to branch out in directions that would normally seem completely alien to you. Go for it!

• *Thursday 23 October* •

As a Water sign you're blessed with considerable creativity and from today you'll really enjoy expressing it in any way you can. You might decide to embark on a new artistic project if you don't have anything on the go at the moment, or you may be creative in a more general sense than usual. Don't forget there are many ways to be creative, including cooking, gardening and even having babies!

• *Friday 24 October* •

You'll thoroughly enjoy using your brain over the next couple of weeks. That could mean immersing yourself in a gripping book that you can hardly bear to put down, testing your IQ with some puzzles or entering every competition you can lay your hands on. Speaking of hands, you'll especially enjoy doing artistic things with them, such as sewing or painting.

• *Saturday 25 October* •

Today's New Moon will bring you some fabulous luck between now and early November. You could hear some very good news about a loved one and possibly even about the birth of a child. If you enjoy gambling you could strike lucky now, although that isn't a licence to bet more than you can afford to lose. And you might even fall in love with someone. A fabulous time awaits you!

• *Sunday 26 October* •

You're feeling very capable today and will enjoy taking things in your stride. If you're with a loved one you'll want to support them in any way you can, whether that means lending them your physical help or giving them your moral support. It's also a good day for teaching children how to do something fun, such as ride a bike or use a skateboard.

• *Monday 27 October* •

Are you feeling OK? It's just that you've probably got steam coming out of both ears and are hopping mad. It's one of those days when people get under your skin in no time at all, irritating you beyond measure and making you grit your teeth. What exactly is going on and why are you so annoyed? You may find that things just escalate, making it hard for you to control your temper.

• *Tuesday 28 October* •

You'll love rising to a challenge today, and the more testing it is, the more excited you'll be. You might even try to talk someone else into doing it with you, and you'll probably succeed because you're nicely persuasive right now. It's certainly a fabulous day for putting across your point of view, particularly if you're trying to stand your ground or justify your actions.

• *Wednesday 29 October* •

No matter what else is going on in your life at the moment, you're in a good mood today. You're feeling positive and cheerful, and as a result everyone else will feel great because your good feelings will rub off on them. If you're currently getting to know someone new, your relationship will progress by leaps and bounds today simply because you're enjoying one another's company so much.

• *Thursday 30 October* •

Keep your wits about you when handling your finances today because someone may be trying to do the dirty on you. Even if they aren't and are simply in a muddle or have got their facts wrong, you may soon feel very suspicious of them and their motives. Watch out if you're already wondering what a loved one is up – your imagination will run riot now, but do you have any facts to back up your fears?

• *Friday 31 October* •

You end the month on a high note and are keen to enjoy yourself whenever you get the chance. It's a super day for spending some money and you won't need any encouragement, either. It's also great for getting together with some of your favourite people. Or perhaps you have a certain person in mind and want to spend as much time with them as possible while making the rest of the world go away?

NOVEMBER AT A GLANCE

Love	❤ ❤ ❤ ❤
Money	£ $
Career	💻 💻 💻 💻 💻
Health	☼ ☼ ☼ ☼ ☼

• *Saturday 1 November* •

You have some very constructive comments to make today, so don't be shy about saying what you think. You'll be able to combine optimism and caution in equal measure, so there is little danger that you'll be falsely confident about something or unduly pessimistic. This is therefore an excellent day for reaching decisions or putting your thoughts down on paper.

• *Sunday 2 November* •

Until late November you'll enjoy being of service to others and putting yourself at their disposal. This might mean doing some favours for someone or looking after them if they're ill. You'll also be at pains to get on well with colleagues and clients. Of course, it will be easy to hit it off with people you already like; the challenge will be to deal with those people who set your teeth on edge, but you'll do your best.

• *Monday 3 November* •

You're in a fantastic mood today, even though it's Monday. With luck, you've got something nice on the agenda, but even if you haven't you'll still want to make the most of the day. It's great for taking yourself on a mini adventure or for doing something that you've never attempted before. Think about what you're doing for Christmas and consider expanding on your existing plans if they aren't very inspiring.

• *Tuesday 4 November* •

Take care of yourself today because you could easily feel under pressure. Perhaps you've got more work than you know what to do with or you're having to cope with a very tricky work-mate. If you want to ask for some time off work, this isn't a very good day to do it because you may not get the answer you are hoping for. You might even arouse someone's jealousy or antagonism.

• *Wednesday 5 November* •

You're capable of tremendous attention to detail today, especially when it comes to projects that allow you to express yourself. You'll enjoy working hard on them and devoting as much time and energy to them as possible. This is also an excellent chance to strengthen your relationship with some of the people in your life. You may even be asked to give one of them some moral support.

• *Thursday 6 November* •

Someone's feeling very expansive and cheerful today! It's a joy to be near them because they're such fantastic company. And the good news is that this person might be you! If it is, you'll still have a lot of fun being with other people now. Any sort of social event will more than live up to its promise and it might even introduce you to a new romantic interest in your life.

• *Friday 7 November* •

Do something inventive or unusual today. You feel like breaking out slightly from your usual routine or way of doing things, and it will be like a breath of fresh air. It may even inspire you with some brilliant ideas that might never have dawned on you otherwise. If you've been wrestling with some red tape you could get an unexpected break now.

• *Saturday 8 November* •

Have you neglected a hobby recently, perhaps because you got slightly bored with it or because of lack of time? If you have, this is a good day for picking up the threads of it again and seeing if you feel any differently about it. You might realize that you've really missed it and that you're glad to start it again, or you may decide that it's still of little interest to you. Try it and see.

• *Sunday 9 November* •

It's time to examine your long-term hopes and wishes, and to see if they're still on track for success. During the coming couple of weeks, think long and hard about all those items on your wish list. How many of them are on there through sheer habit? Maybe something that you have dreamed of is now less of a priority and other ambitions have taken its place? If so, recognize this fact and make any adjustments that are necessary.

• *Monday 10 November* •

Joint and official money matters don't exactly run smoothly today. You might have to cope with some unexpected developments or someone may go out of their way to make life difficult for you. It doesn't help that you'll have to reckon with interruptions and moments when things go wrong. It's a day that will try your patience.

• *Tuesday 11 November* •

You have a big heart, as is more than obvious today. You're in a very generous mood and will want to make loved ones feel cherished and wanted. It's a terrific day for making a big fuss of a special person and having a big fuss made of you in return. If something romantic is brewing between you and a colleague or someone you've met through a work or health matter, today's events will boost your confidence.

• *Wednesday 12 November* •

You won't like it if you feel your free time is being encroached upon today, and will want to stand up for yourself at every opportunity. This may make you seem rather aggressive and defensive, because you're so quick to take offence. Do your best to keep things in proportion and don't allow your feelings to run away with you.

• *Thursday 13 November* •

You're rather self-contained and withdrawn today, making you come across as shy and reserved. You definitely want to keep yourself to yourself right now, but try not to give the impression that you're being stand-offish or awkward. You're also feeling quite strict with yourself and may forbid yourself any nice treats, such as a bar of chocolate or an extra biscuit. Strong-willed or what!

• *Friday 14 November* •

You're capable of achieving a great deal today, especially if you can combine your will power with your powers of organization. Certain people may find you rather formidable, and you certainly shouldn't use today's energies to intimidate anyone or boss them about. Instead, enjoy the sense that you're doing your best and that everything is falling into place.

• *Saturday 15 November* •

If you're going to a social event today you'll want to have a whale of a time. You won't care about breaking your diet or having that extra drink, or whatever else seems like a naughty treat to you. Mind you, you may wish you hadn't been quite so unrestrained tomorrow morning when you wake up with a sore head! In the meantime, however, you are delighted by any excuse to let your hair down.

• *Sunday 16 November* •

If you're near the shops today you'll enjoy buying items that make you feel or look good. It's even better if they will boost your health or well-being in some way. For instance, you might be tempted by some delicious foods that are supposed to be healthy, or you could decide to buy some bottles of

vitamins or minerals. They may not be very exciting but you'll
be perfectly happy with them!

• *Monday 17 November* •

Watch out today because a certain someone doesn't know
when to mind their own business. They may stick their nose
into things that are nothing to do with them, and then get on
their high horse when they don't like what you're doing. It
will be a miracle if you manage to get through the day without
losing your temper with someone at some point, especially if
they seem jealous or possessive of you. Tricky.

• *Tuesday 18 November* •

A workmate has very definite ideas about how they want
things to be, and they'll probably sulk if they don't get their
own way. They'll be about as subtle as a Scud missile over this,
so you'll definitely get the hint. Yet that will make you even
more resolute about standing your ground and not being
swayed by what you see as childish tactics. But make sure
you don't descend to this level yourself.

• *Wednesday 19 November* •

You're in a very sunny temper today and you want to spread
your good humour in as many directions as possible. Today's
fabulous for getting together with some of the special people
in your life, particularly if you're doing something that you
really enjoy. It's an especially happy time if you're with you-
know-who, in which case you won't really mind what you're
doing provided you can be together.

• *Thursday 20 November* •

Try not to over-reach yourself today, especially if you're doing
something that requires guts or courage. Although it's a

fantastic opportunity to push yourself further than usual, you nevertheless need to slam on the brakes before you go over the top or do something that you'll really regret later on. Be particularly careful not to do anything that could physically injure you, such as straining a muscle.

• *Friday 21 November* •

Someone needs as much independence and freedom as you can possibly give them today. Even though every nerve in your body is telling you to hold on tightly to this person, this will be a recipe for disaster because it will make them want to run in the opposite direction as fast as their legs can carry them. They may even create a huge and unpleasant scene, so be careful.

• *Saturday 22 November* •

Between now and this time next month you'll want to do the best you can at work. If there are tasks or projects that you want to complete by Christmas or the end of the year, you'll be in a good position to do so because you'll pull out all the stops if necessary. It will also be a good time to take more notice of your health, particularly if you've been neglecting yourself recently or you feel you're running on empty.

• *Sunday 23 November* •

You've got some great ideas today, especially if you're coming up with plans connected to your work or your daily routine. You're thinking big right now, which is just what's needed, provided you know when to call a halt. This is also an excellent chance to discuss your point of view if you've recently had a difference of opinion with someone. You'll have no qualms about putting across your side of the story.

• *Monday 24 November* •

It's awfully easy to speak out of turn today and to drop a massive clanger. You may even offend someone, if you're really unlucky. Alternatively, it may be you who's drawing in your breath sharply because you don't like what someone has said. If so, ask yourself what you are so annoyed about. Have they really trampled on your finer feelings, or is there some other reason for your current anger?

• *Tuesday 25 November* •

You have such strong powers of concentration today that it's the ideal opportunity to go over anything in fine detail. You might want to check some work that you've done recently, write a complicated letter or do something that requires tremendous manual dexterity. Your curiosity may also be aroused now, perhaps by what a colleague is getting up to or by a health mystery that needs uncovering.

• *Wednesday 26 November* •

Someone is on the warpath today, so watch your back. They aren't taking any prisoners and they aren't listening to sense either. They're imposing their ideas on you, and if you resist them it could swiftly become a battle of wills. The key to this is to know when to stand your ground and when to exercise moderation. Above all, try not to be drawn into anything that threatens to get out of hand.

• *Thursday 27 November* •

Harmony rules in your relationships between now and late December. That will make a refreshing change after all the skirmishes of the past few days! Of course, you may still have run-ins with people but you will do your utmost to end them as soon as possible and to resolve them amicably. Even so, there could be times when you have to stand your ground despite the ructions this causes.

• *Friday 28 November* •

Colleagues are very amenable today and you'll get on well with them. If you're hoping that your relationship with a certain workmate will soon stop being professional and become sexual or romantic instead, what happens now will give you fresh hope. If you're feeling brave, how about asking them out for a drink or at least chatting them up?

• *Saturday 29 November* •

You're feeling organized today and will get a lot of satisfaction from checking that all the minutiae of your life are running smoothly. You might decide to check that your insurance policies are still offering you good value, or that your savings accounts are providing the best rate of interest. If necessary, pick someone's brains about what they would recommend.

• *Sunday 30 November* •

Oh dear. Someone is being awfully touchy today, making you wonder what on earth you can do to avoid getting it in the neck from them. Perhaps your best bet is to confront them sooner rather than later, and ask what's wrong. If you can feel steam starting to shoot out of your own ears, try to do something about it before you reach screaming point because that won't do you, or anyone else, any good at all.

DECEMBER AT A GLANCE

Love	♥ ♥ ♥ ♥ ♥
Money	£ $ £
Career	💻 💻 💻 💻 💻
Health	☼ ☼ ☼ ☼ ☼

• *Monday 1 December* •

Whatever else is going on in your life, you're determined to make the best of it today. You may even resolve to put any problems to the back of your mind because you don't want them to ruin your day. On a different tack, this is a great day to increase your knowledge of the world in some way. You might decide to learn something new or possibly even enrol in a course or class starting next January.

• *Tuesday 2 December* •

One of the best ways to get on well with others at the moment is to take great care in your communications with them. You know what muddles we all get into if we misunderstand each other, but this is a lot less likely for you during the rest of the month. Do your best to be very clear and straightforward when talking to other people, and to check that you understand what they are talking about in return.

• *Wednesday 3 December* •

The atmosphere at work is very good today, enabling you to get on with things to the best of your ability. If you're taking part in a meeting or discussion, you'll be able to put across your ideas and may even earn a pat on the back for some of them. Your relationship with your boss or any other authority figure looks good now, and you're also able to keep on the right side of colleagues. Great!

• *Thursday 4 December* •

You have all sorts of good ideas today, especially if they're slightly unusual or even a complete departure from the way your mind normally works. Don't feel threatened or worried by this. Instead, use it to your advantage because you could come up with some wonderful schemes. You may also hit on the answer to a long-running problem simply by viewing it from a different angle.

• *Friday 5 December* •

Have you started writing your Christmas cards yet? If you shudder at the very thought, try to set aside time today to buy them and then begin writing them. You'll soon get into the mood and may even be inspired to write a few letters as well. Any other Christmas preparations will benefit from your time and effort now, but don't forget to do something sociable or enjoyable at some point.

• *Saturday 6 December* •

There's a chill in the air today and it's got nothing to do with the weather. Instead, it's caused by the sense of distance and reserve between you and a certain person. You may even experience this as a yawning chasm between you, making you wonder if you will ever bridge it. Try not to imagine that things are worse than they really are, or to protect yourself by being off-hand and cool. That may make the other person think you don't care about what happens to your relationship.

• *Sunday 7 December* •

You're full of bounce and energy today, and you want to do something exciting. It's no good doing the same old Sunday things as usual if they always make you feel slightly bored or fed up, because you'll soon get restless. How about doing some Christmas shopping in another town or getting in the car for a mystery tour?

• *Monday 8 December* •

If something has been nagging away at you and making you feel worried or uncomfortable, try to take constructive action over the coming fortnight. If you can't change the situation, perhaps you can alter your attitude towards it? Even talking things through with someone will help you to feel better because you'll be able to express some of your feelings.

• *Tuesday 9 December* •

A certain person is in a bad mood today, and don't you know it! They're breathing fire and you get the distinct impression that they're expecting you to tiptoe around them. But are you prepared to do this? If it's an all-too-familiar story, you may prefer to carry on as usual and let them like it or lump it. If you're lucky, this sort of bravado may even make them come to their senses and stop behaving like a child.

• *Wednesday 10 December* •

Someone is awfully full of themselves today. You suspect that they're getting too big for their boots, particularly if you encounter them through work. Maybe they think they've got all the answers or they want you to know how important they are. Without realizing it, you may also be giving this impression, perhaps because you're taking things in your stride or you seem very competent and confident.

• *Thursday 11 December* •

If you're going to a seasonal party today you'll have a whale of a time. It's exactly what you're in the mood for, and you'll want to be as scintillating as possible. It's a good excuse to dress up in some of your best clothes because you never know who you might meet. Besides, it will do you good to know you're looking a knockout.

• *Friday 12 December* •

This is an excellent day for changing any systems, routines or arrangements that have got stale or are no longer working. However, if you're wise you'll check your plans with the other people concerned first, purely out of courtesy if nothing else. You won't get very far if you try to impose your ideas on others or, even worse, bully them into submission. You'll only encounter opposition that way.

• *Saturday 13 December* •

Your opinion of yourself is trailing round your ankles today. Why is this? Is it because you suspect that a certain person doesn't think much of you at the moment, or is it because you currently have such high standards that only a saint could live up to them? Although it's good to keep yourself up to the mark, don't become despondent if you realize you're only human. Just do the best you can.

• *Sunday 14 December* •

You need a break today. It will do you the world of good, especially if you've been working away like mad all week. Even if you have the misfortune of being at work today, make sure you do as little as possible once you get home. Put your feet up, go to bed early, or lock the bathroom door and soak in the bath for an hour. You'll soon start to feel restored.

• *Monday 15 December* •

It's good fun keeping in contact with people today. You might spend a lot of time on the phone to people or you may prefer to see them in person. If you're still busy with your Christmas preparations, you'll enjoy going shopping or writing cards today. If you're wrapping presents, you'll put a lot of effort into them.

• *Tuesday 16 December* •

Your ambitions get a massive shot in the arm today, and during the next couple of months you'll want to push full steam ahead with your goals and aims. What's more, you won't be pleased if you meet delays or stumbling blocks along the way. If you feel you've been sidelined at work or you haven't received the credit that you think is due to you, you'll be very miffed and will feel resentful.

• *Wednesday 17 December* •

Over the next couple of weeks it won't always be easy to understand what people want from you. They may be saying one thing while sending you covert messages that say something very different, or they might keep changing their minds. This isn't a good time to enter into any sort of agreement with someone, whether verbal or on paper, because one of you may have overlooked some salient facts.

• *Thursday 18 December* •

Someone dear to your heart is very hoity-toity today. They're easily offended and as a result are quick to leap to their own defence, imagining that you're getting at them or impugning their good name. Even if you aren't doing anything so dastardly, you may unconsciously be winding them up and trying to get a rise out of them. Anything connected with their past or family will be particularly tricky now.

• *Friday 19 December* •

You're not afraid of hard work today, which is just as well if there's a lot to sort out before you start your Christmas holidays. In fact, you'll take pride in doing whatever is necessary to clear the decks. Keep a lookout for your colleagues because you may have to mother or comfort one of them who's going through a rough patch at the moment.

• *Saturday 20 December* •

If you're trying to get all your last-minute Christmas shopping out of the way, you'll come up with some very good ideas now. You're full of common sense and may even be able to solve other people's gift problems as well as your own. It pays to think ahead now and you might decide to buy some extra presents to put under the tree, just in case someone gives you a surprise gift.

• *Sunday 21 December* •

It pays to get intimate with people during the next few weeks! You'll enjoy cuddling up close to someone very special and possibly even rediscovering all the reasons why you got together in the first place. Even if sex is out of the question for some reason, you'll want to establish a greater closeness and understanding with people now. This means opening your heart and revealing your true self, but it's something that you're ready to do.

• *Monday 22 December* •

Is someone making you doubt your abilities today? They seem to be giving you the impression that they think you're stupid or that you can't think for yourself, even though that's nonsense. Ask yourself why you think they're being so tough on you. You may decide that the whole situation has more to do with your own fears than with anything concrete that's happened. Perhaps you're worrying about nothing?

• Tuesday 23 December •

Today's New Moon is casting a spell over your relationships and reminding you of all that can be gained from improving your partnerships during the next two weeks. If you've been at daggers drawn with someone recently, this is a marvellous opportunity to set aside your differences and to start afresh. You may also be about to meet someone new, which will be very exciting.

• Wednesday 24 December •

Although it's the season to be jolly, you're looking rather down in the mouth today. What's wrong? Perhaps you're worried about not having everything ready in time for tomorrow, you're anxious about someone's welfare, or you simply don't feel very festive. It's one of those days when it's easy to let things get on top of you but try not to let this happen. Instead, maintain some objectivity.

• Thursday 25 December •

You're feeling so much better than you did yesterday and you want to enjoy yourself as much as possible. You'll make a special fuss of older friends and relatives, hoping that they have a good day and they're included in everything that's going on. It's also nice for being with your beloved and having some private time together. After all, you don't want that mistletoe to go to waste, do you?

• *Friday 26 December* •

The mood is a little strained today. Someone may be getting agitated and snapping at everyone who is foolish enough to speak to them. Unfortunately it's the sort of atmosphere that's very infectious, so before you know where you are there may be rows breaking out in all directions. If you start to get angry yourself, try to deal with the situation as rationally as possible and don't allow yourself to get out of control.

• *Saturday 27 December* •

If you think you stepped out of line yesterday you now have the chance to say sorry. With luck, everything will have blown over and you'll all be feeling much calmer. It's a lovely day for catching up with people you haven't seen over the past few days. You might even fancy throwing an impromptu party for your friends or neighbours.

• *Sunday 28 December* •

You need a big pinch of salt today because someone is stretching the truth almost to breaking point. They're exaggerating so much that it's laughable, but you feel quite good-natured about it. It's a good day to go for a long walk, especially if you take someone along for company, but don't be surprised if they suggest turning it into a route march. You may arrive home bedraggled and exhausted!

• *Monday 29 December* •

Someone's operating on a short fuse today, so take care. They're feeling argumentative and pernickety, and are inclined to argue the toss at every opportunity. This will be tiresome and irritating, especially if you're drawn into having a row. Maybe you need some time on your own?

• *Tuesday 30 December* •

The post-Christmas holidays are turning out to be rather a pain, because yet again you have to cope with someone who's got themselves into a right old state. Perhaps you should ask them what's wrong, because they may have very real reasons for being so angry or restless. Even so, all is not lost because it's a great day for planning some of your New Year resolutions. Write them down in your new diary so you won't forget them.

• *Wednesday 31 December* •

You're feeling very conscientious today and won't rest until you've completed everything you set out to do. Try not to make a rod for your own back by taking on more than you can manage or more than is necessary, simply because you don't want anyone to think you're slacking or not pulling your weight. Besides, you don't want to be so tired that you can't greet 2004 in style!

YOUR CANCER SUN SIGN

In this chapter I am going to tell you all about your Cancerian Sun sign. But what is a Sun sign? It often gets called a star sign, but are they the same thing? Well, yes, although 'Sun sign' is a more accurate term. Your Sun sign is the sign that the Sun occupied when you were born. Every year, the Sun moves through the heavens and spends an average of 30 days in each of the twelve signs. When you were born, the Sun was moving through the sign of Cancer, so this is your Sun or star sign.

This chapter tells you everything you want to know about your Sun sign. To start off, I describe your general personality – what makes you tick. Then I talk about your attitude to relationships, the way you handle money, what your Sun sign says about your health and, finally, which careers are best for you. Put all that together and you will have a well-rounded picture of yourself.

 Character

Cancer is the first of the three Water signs, which means you're very compassionate, sensitive and affectionate. You feel an instinctive urge to take care of other people – and sometimes you'll do it whether they want this or not! You like to tuck loved ones under your wing and protect them. You may also secretly believe that a hot meal can soothe many ills. After all, you are the cook of the zodiac!

Anything connected with home comforts is a winner for you. Your world probably revolves around your home and family. If you aren't in contact with your own kith and kin for some reason, you like to create your own family from friends. Home is definitely where your heart is, and you'll always feel a sense of relief when you walk through your front door and return to your familiar territory.

You belong to the sign of the Crab and you share the crustacean's strong defences against the rest of the world. The crab has his hard shell, and you can also come across as being rather tough and well protected at times. When you feel people are trying to get at you, you may even decide that attack is the best form of defence. Unfortunately, this can sometimes mean that you make situations more difficult than they need be.

You are very tenacious and don't like giving up. You also don't like admitting defeat, so can hold on to situations long after you should have walked away from them.

Relationships

You can't imagine not having other people in your life. Who would you take care of, for a start? You love to look after people and you instinctively respond to them with sympathy and compassion. One of your favourite ways of showing that you care is to feed people! It gives you great pleasure to cook someone a meal or bake them a cake, for no other reason than that you want to make them feel good.

Because you have such a strong need for emotional security,

you're often reluctant to let partners out of your sight for long. Perhaps you're worried that they won't come back? Although you simply enjoy their company, occasionally they can feel rather smothered, so it's important for you to give them plenty of room to breathe. Be especially careful not to place heavy emotional demands on your loved ones, or to use emotional blackmail. It's often difficult for you to be direct when asking for things that you need, and this can often be misunderstood by others.

You're the sort of person who wants a relationship to last for ever, so you can be resistant to the idea of endings. Your instincts may tell you to hold on to a relationship long after it should have finished but this can lead to unhappiness and stop you moving forward. When dealing with problems in a relationship, you find it hard to talk about what's wrong. You hope that your partner will somehow read your mind and prevent you having to put things into words.

Money

You have an instinctive respect for money and what it can buy. As a result, you're very careful about what you spend your money on and you're one of the canniest investors in the zodiac. For a start, you'll want to put your money into bricks and mortar long before your contemporaries. You don't feel entirely secure until you've got a roof over your head. When buying a home, you'll use your instincts to tell you whether it's right for you or not, and you will also back your hunches when considering other forms of investment. If you get a strong urge to buy something or to choose one building society rather than another, you should go with your instincts unless there are very good reasons against doing this.

If you're looking for interesting investments, other than the usual options, you might consider antiques and silver. These are both ruled by Cancer so you'll get more pleasure from them than your building society passbook!

Health

You're so intuitive and sensitive that you easily absorb the atmosphere around you. That's great when you're in happy, easy surroundings because you feel really good. But it can be a problem if you're with people who are agitated, angry or depressed because you might pick up their mood in no time at all. It's therefore important that you find ways of protecting yourself from other people's emotions when these threaten to disturb your own.

The sign of Cancer rules the stomach and breasts, so you need to take particular care of these areas of your anatomy. Your stomach can easily react to difficult situations, either by becoming upset or by feeling like a cage full of butterflies. Learning relaxation techniques will help and you may also find it useful to alter your diet and avoid any foods that make the situation worse.

Because you're a Water sign, your emotions tend to rule your life and you need to find techniques that stop you becoming het up and fraught. One good way to do this is to surround yourself with water. Having a fragrant soak in the bath is one answer, or you might go swimming regularly. Walking beside a river, lake or ocean can also help you to unwind when things get on top of you.

Career

If you want a career that makes the most of your natural abilities, anything that involves caring is an obvious choice. You might do this through nursing, for instance, or by being a care worker. Children are a particular love of many Cancerians, so you may enjoy being a teacher, a nanny or working in a nursery.

Food is another area where you come into your own. How about working in the catering business, whether you run a restaurant, wait at tables or cook the food? Or perhaps you're drawn to the idea of working in a hotel, where you can welcome people and make them feel at home?

Antiques have a big appeal for many Cancerians, so you might enjoy working in an antiques shop or for an auctioneer's. You may also have a great interest in history, so you might enjoy studying the subject or teaching it. Professions connected with water can also appeal to you.

Whichever way you earn your daily bread, you'll want to do it in congenial surroundings. You'll also enjoy making a big fuss of your colleagues, perhaps bringing in home-made biscuits or cakes for special occasions (such as every Friday!) or instigating regular evenings when you all go out for a meal so you can get to know one another better.

LOVE AND THE STARS

Have you ever noticed that you get on better with some signs than others? Perhaps all your friends belong to only a few signs or you've never hit it off with people who come from a particular sign. Or maybe you've recently met someone from a sign that you aren't familiar with at all, and you're wondering how your relationship will develop. Well, this chapter gives you a brief insight into your relationship with the other Sun signs. Check the combination under your own sign's heading first, then read about your relationship from the viewpoint of the other sign to find out what they think of you. It could be very revealing!

At the end of this chapter you'll find two compatibility charts that tell you, at a glance, how well you get on with the other signs as lovers and as friends. Look for the woman's Sun sign along the top of the chart and then find the man's sign down the side. The box where the two meet will show how well they get on together.

Even if your current relationship gets a low score from the charts, that doesn't mean it won't last. It simply indicates that you'll have to work harder at this relationship than at others.

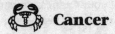 **Cancer**

Cancer and **Cancer** is wonderful because you're able to take refuge in each other. You'll lavish a lot of time and effort on your home. Problems will arise if one of you doesn't get on well with the other one's family or friends.

Cancer and **Leo** share a love of family life, and you may even agree to give it priority over everything else. You'll be very proud of your Leo's achievements but will fret if these take them away from home too often.

Cancer and **Virgo** have a lot to teach each other. You'll learn from your Virgo how to do things methodically and carefully, and you'll encourage them to be more demonstrative and loving. It should work well!

Cancer and **Libra** is great if you have shared goals. You both understand the importance of ambition and will readily support one another. You enjoy being with someone who isn't afraid to show their affections.

Cancer and **Scorpio** is a very emotional and satisfying pairing. You know you can reveal your true feelings to your Scorpio, and you'll encourage them to do the same with you. Sexually, you'll really be in your element.

Cancer and **Sagittarius** find it hard to appreciate each other. You may even feel as though you come from different planets because you operate on a very emotional level while your Sagittarian prefers to stick to the facts.

Cancer and **Capricorn** is a case of opposites attracting. You both need what the other one can offer, and you'll be especially pleased if your Capricorn's capacity for hard work will provide a roof over your head and a stable home.

Cancer and **Aquarius** can be quirky friends but you'll struggle to sustain an emotional relationship because you're chalk and cheese. Your need for love and reassurance may be very difficult for your Aquarian to deal with.

Cancer and **Pisces** are really happy together. It's great knowing that you're with someone who understands your deep emotional needs and your complicated personality. You'll also revel in taking care of your Piscean.

Cancer and **Aries** can work if you both make allowances for each other. You need to give your Aries a lot of freedom because they'll get very angry if they feel they're tied to your apron strings.

Cancer and **Taurus** is a marriage made in heaven. You both need a happy, comfortable home and you also share a love of food. Your relationship may be so self-sufficient that you barely need anyone else in your lives.

Cancer and **Gemini** is OK if you don't spend too much time together! You'll feel slightly threatened by your Gemini's need for an active and independent social life, and they'll resent being expected to spend so much time at home.

 Leo

Leo and **Leo** is a very strong combination but there could be a few battles for power every now and then. After all, neither of you likes to relinquish the reins and hand over control to anyone else. Even so, you'll have a lot of fun.

Leo and **Virgo** is fine if you're prepared for some give and take but it won't be very easy if each of you stands your ground. You'll be pleased if your Virgo tries to help or advise you, but will be hurt if this turns to undue criticism.

Leo and **Libra** is a delicious pairing because it brings together the two signs of love. You'll adore being with someone who is so considerate, although their lack of decisiveness may sometimes make you grit your teeth with irritation.

Leo and **Scorpio** is wonderful until you have a row. At that point, you'll both refuse to budge an inch and admit that you might be in the wrong. You both set a lot of store by status symbols, which could work out expensive.

Leo and **Sagittarius** is great for keeping each other amused. You're both enthusiastic, intuitive and expansive, although you could sometimes be annoyed if your Sagittarian's social life prevents you seeing much of them.

Leo and **Capricorn** share a tremendous love of family and you'll enjoy creating a happy home together. Don't expect your Capricorn to be instinctively demonstrative: you may have to teach them to be more open.

Leo and **Aquarius** understand each other even if you don't always see eye to eye. Sometimes you can be left speechless by your plain-speaking Aquarian, and disappointed by their occasional reluctance to be cuddly.

Leo and **Pisces** bring out each other's creativity. This is a superb artistic partnership but may not be such good news if you're trying to maintain a sexual relationship because you have so little in common.

Leo and **Aries** have terrific fun together and will share many adventures. You'll enjoy making lots of plans, even if they don't always work out. You'll also spend plenty of money on lavishly entertaining your friends.

Leo and **Taurus** is the sort of relationship that makes you feel you know where you stand. You love knowing that your Taurean is steadfast and true, and that together you make a formidable team.

Leo and **Gemini** is a fun-filled combination that you really enjoy. You're stunned by your Gemini's endless inventiveness and their versatility, although you may secretly believe that they spread themselves too thin.

Leo and **Cancer** is great if you both need a comfortable and cosy home. But you may soon feel hemmed in if your Cancerian wants to restrict your social circle to nothing but family and close friends. You need more scope than that.

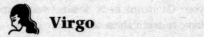 **Virgo**

Virgo and **Virgo** can endure many storms together, even though it's tough going at times. Here is someone who completely understands your interesting mixture of quirky individualism and the need to conform.

Virgo and **Libra** get on well together up to a point but can then come unstuck. It annoys you when your Libran fails to stand up for themselves and you don't understand why they're so touchy when you point out their faults.

Virgo and **Scorpio** are both fascinated by the details of life and you'll spend many happy hours analysing people's characters. Try not to be too brusque when pointing out some of your Scorpio's stranger points; they won't like it!

Virgo and **Sagittarius** is a very sociable pairing and you'll enjoy being together. You'll also have some fascinating conversations in which you both learn a lot. Sexually, it will either be great or ghastly.

Virgo and **Capricorn** really understand each other. You appreciate your Capricorn's reliability but worry about their workaholic tendencies. You'll both benefit from being openly affectionate and loving with one another.

Virgo and **Aquarius** enjoy discussing just about everything under the sun. But you'll quickly get irritated by your Aquarian's idiosyncratic views and their insistence that they're always right. Surely if anyone's right, you are?

Virgo and **Pisces** is not the easiest combination you can choose. If your Piscean finds it hard to face up to reality, you won't be sympathetic because you simply can't understand such an ostrich-like attitude.

Virgo and **Aries** struggle to get on well as close partners. You simply don't understand each other. They make a mess and you like things to be tidy. They rush into things and you like to take your time. There is little common ground.

Virgo and **Taurus** love each other's company. You both like to keep your feet on the ground and you share a healthy respect for money. You also have a very raunchy time in the bedroom although you don't advertise that fact.

Virgo and **Gemini** is a super combination for friendship or business. You think along similar lines and both excel at being flexible. However, in a sexual relationship you may fail to appreciate each other's finer points.

Virgo and **Cancer** is a great team. You like to take care of worldly matters while your Cancerian creates a happy and cosy home. If they collect a lot of clutter you'll think of it as dust traps rather than delightful keepsakes.

Virgo and **Leo** find it hard to understand each other because you're so different. You may secretly find your Leo rather ostentatious and there could be rows about the amount of money they spend. Try to live and let live.

 Libra

Libra and **Libra** get on really well provided at least one of you is decisive and able to say what they think sometimes. You'll appreciate one another's consideration, sensitivity and intelligence. A great combination!

Libra and **Scorpio** are good friends but may not understand each other's sexual and emotional needs. You may feel uncomfortable with the brooding, intense moods of your Scorpio, wishing they took things less seriously.

Libra and **Sagittarius** have lots of fun together, especially when it comes to discussing ideas and taking off on jaunts.

However, you could be rather nonplussed, and possibly even hurt, by your Sagittarian's blunt comments.

Libra and **Capricorn** get on famously if you share goals. You understand each other's need to work hard towards your ambitions. But you'll have to coax your Capricorn into being as demonstrative and loving as you'd like.

Libra and **Aquarius** appreciate one another's minds. You may be better friends than lovers, because you could be bemused and hurt if your Aquarian is unnerved by your need for romance and idealism.

Libra and **Pisces** share a need for peace and harmony. You'll adore being with someone who's so artistic and sensitive, but you both need to balance your romantic natures with hefty doses of reality every now and then.

Libra and **Aries** are a great example of how opposites can attract. You admire the way your brave Arien can be so outspoken, and they may even manage to teach you to stand up for yourself.

Libra and **Taurus** share a love of beauty and an appreciation of the finer things in life. At first you may think you've found your perfect partner, although you may get irritated if your Taurean is very placid.

Libra and **Gemini** get on well in every sort of relationship. You're amused by your Gemini's butterfly ability to flit from one topic to the next and will enjoy encouraging them to discover the romance that lurks inside them.

Libra and **Cancer** enjoy one another's company. You love the way your Cancerian so obviously cares about your welfare and happiness, and it does you good to be the one who's fussed over for a change.

Libra and **Leo** can be a very expensive combination! Neither of you is frightened to spend money and together you can have a field day. Emotionally, you revel in one another's company because you're both born romantics.

Libra and **Virgo** have to make a lot of effort to appreciate one another. You can understand the importance of attending to details but you may secretly think that your Virgo sometimes is too much of a nit-picker.

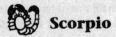 **Scorpio**

Scorpio and **Scorpio** feel safe with each other. You both know what you're capable of, good and bad. It's great to be with someone who matches you for intensity, but you might wind each other up and feed each other's neuroses.

Scorpio and **Sagittarius** can miss each other by miles. Even as friends, it's hard to understand one another. You like to zero in on the details while your Sagittarian prefers to take a broad view of the entire situation.

Scorpio and **Capricorn** bring out the best in one another, but it can take a little time. You enjoy the serious side to your Capricorn but you can also have some great laughs together. You also love knowing that they're so reliable.

Scorpio and **Aquarius** can have some terrific rows! You both have a tendency to be dogmatic and it's even worse when you get together. You can feel threatened if your Aquarian isn't as openly affectionate as you'd like.

Scorpio and **Pisces** share some powerful moments together. You love the complexity and sensitivity of your Piscean but will soon become suspicious if you think they're holding out on you or are playing games behind your back.

Scorpio and **Aries** is a tempestuous combination. Your temper builds up from a slow burn while your Arien will have a quick tantrum and then forget about it. Sexually, you'll have more than met your match.

Scorpio and **Taurus** complement each other in many ways. You're both loyal and loving, and you both need a secure home. However, problems will arise if one or both of you is possessive and jealous.

Scorpio and **Gemini** hit it off as friends but will struggle to stick together as lovers. You like to explore the nitty-gritty of situations while your Gemini apparently prefers to skim the surface. You may wonder if you can trust them.

Scorpio and **Cancer** can enjoy a highly emotional and satisfying relationship. You understand one another's needs and will take great delight in creating a stable and happy home life together.

Scorpio and **Leo** is tricky if you both want to rule the roost. Neither of you likes to relinquish control of situations, which can lead to some stormy battles for power. At times you may be jealous of your Leo's huge circle of friends.

Scorpio and **Virgo** have some wonderfully analytical conversations. You both enjoy digging below the surface to find out what's really going on. If it's a sexual relationship, its success will rest on what happens in the bedroom.

Scorpio and **Libra** appreciate one another but you may sometimes wish your Libran could be more forceful and dynamic. It will drive you mad when they sit on the fence or bend over backwards to please everyone.

♐ Sagittarius

Sagittarius and **Sagittarius** will either have a whale of a time or never see each other. If you both have wide-ranging interests, it may be difficult to make enough time for one another and you may eventually drift apart.

Sagittarius and **Capricorn** think of each other as a creature from another planet. You like your Capricorn's common sense but will soon get fed up if they cling to tradition, are a workaholic or never want to take any risks.

Sagittarius and **Aquarius** have a fantastic time together. You share so many interests that there is always something to talk about, with some far-ranging discussions. But you may wish your Aquarian were less pedantic.

Sagittarius and **Pisces** enjoy being friends but it can be difficult to understand each other as lovers. You like your Piscean's sensitivity but wish they weren't quite so easily hurt when you make off-the-cuff comments.

Sagittarius and **Aries** is great fun. You'll have all sorts of adventures together, with exotic holidays a particular indulgence. You're both pretty outspoken and your no-holds-barred rows will raise the roof.

Sagittarius and **Taurus** struggle to hit it off. You're so different that it's hard to find much common ground. If your Taurean is possessive, you'll soon feel trapped and want to break free, or decide to do things behind their back.

Sagittarius and **Gemini** is a super combination. You have masses in common and are endlessly intrigued by one another. However, you must be friends as well as lovers, otherwise you may soon get bored with each other.

Sagittarius and **Cancer** can't make each other out at all. You're mystified by your Cancerian's constant need for their home and family, and will be irritated if you think they're too parochial and unadventurous.

Sagittarius and **Leo** revel in each other's company, especially when it comes to having fun. This can be an expensive pairing because you both enjoy living it up whenever you get the chance. Shopping trips will also be costly.

Sagittarius and **Virgo** is OK up to a point. You enjoy each other's brains but you'll soon lose patience if your Virgo is very finicky and anxious. You like to let your hair down but they may always worry about the consequences.

Sagittarius and **Libra** like each other, whether as friends, family or lovers. You have enough similarities to find some common ground but enough differences to keep things interesting. It's an intriguing combination.

Sagittarius and **Scorpio** try and fail to understand each other. You like to take life as it comes and can't stand your Scorpio's tendency to plot things in advance. You'll hate it if they're suspicious or jealous of you.

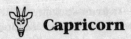

Capricorn

Capricorn and **Capricorn** feel very safe together. At last you're with someone who understands you, and who's as reliable and responsible as you. However, this may mean that your work clashes with your relationship.

Capricorn and **Aquarius** is either a big hit or a big no-no. You both need to compromise and to be willing to learn from each other for it to work. Your love of convention will be sorely challenged by your radical Aquarian.

Capricorn and **Pisces** can learn a lot from each other as friends. You'll learn to be more sensitive and open-minded. However, you'll soon be turned off if your Piscean is reluctant to face up to facts and be realistic.

Capricorn and **Aries** support each other in many ways. You're both ambitious and will respect one another's goals. You'll enjoy teaching your Arien to be more responsible, and they'll teach you how to play.

Capricorn and **Taurus** feel safe with one another. You both understand the importance of tradition and share the need to do things properly. You can get surprisingly earthy and intense in the bedroom.

Capricorn and **Gemini** don't really hit it off. You're amused by your Gemini but you may secretly think they're too flighty and superficial for you. It's difficult to find much common ground sexually or emotionally.

Capricorn and **Cancer** really enjoy each other's company. You both adore having someone to take care of, and if anyone can dissuade you from working round the clock it's a home-cooking, sensuous and affectionate Cancerian.

Capricorn and **Leo** both like the best in life but you won't be as willing to pay for it as your Leo. In fact, you may be seriously worried by their extravagance and also slightly wearied by their demanding social life.

Capricorn and **Virgo** go together like bread and butter. However, there may not be much jam if you're both careful with your money. If you share a home you'll want it to be traditional, with conventional family values.

Capricorn and **Libra** have a healthy respect for each other. You love your Libran's diplomacy and tact, because you know you can take them anywhere and they'll fit in. They'll also encourage you to open up emotionally.

Capricorn and **Scorpio** is a very businesslike pairing. You excel at making money together, no matter what your relationship. Sometimes you can be put off by the intense and complex passions of your Scorpio.

Capricorn and **Sagittarius** can be strange. You like each other for your curiosity value if not much else. Even so, your Sagittarian will teach you to be more broad-minded and relaxed, if you let them.

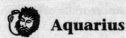 **Aquarius**

Aquarius and **Aquarius** is either wonderful or too much like hard work. One if not both of you must be willing to compromise sometimes, otherwise it will be continual stalemate. You'll have formidable battles of intellect.

Aquarius and **Pisces** is tricky. You don't understand each other, and the more unworldly and unrealistic your Piscean, the more dogmatic and precise you'll become in retaliation. You can easily hurt each other.

Aquarius and **Aries** are great sparring partners and you'll love every minute of it. Your Arien isn't afraid to stand up to you and to fight their corner. They'll also teach you a thing or two about sexual relationships.

Aquarius and **Taurus** is fine all the while you agree with each other. But, at the first hint of dissent, it will be war. Your need for emotional and intellectual freedom will clash with your Taurean's need for closeness.

Aquarius and **Gemini** are firm friends. You enjoy intense intellectual discussions and your Gemini will teach you to be more free-thinking and flexible. Try not to analyse your relationship out of existence.

Aquarius and **Cancer** can be an uneasy combination. You have little in common and don't understand each other. At first you'll enjoy being taken care of by your Cancerian but you may soon feel suffocated and trapped.

Aquarius and **Leo** enjoy each other's company. You love your Leo's exuberance and marvel at their social skills. You'll also be very impressed by their ability to organize you and make your life run so smoothly.

Aquarius and **Virgo** can seem like hard work. It's easier to be friends than lovers because you have such different views of the world. You enjoy pitting your wits against each other in wide-ranging discussions.

Aquarius and **Libra** is great fun and you love sharing ideas. If you get involved in an emotional relationship, your Libran will encourage you to be more demonstrative and less analytical about your feelings.

Aquarius and **Scorpio** is a very powerful combination because you're both so sure of yourselves. In the inevitable disputes, neither of you will want to back down. You may also be turned off by your Scorpio's complicated emotions.

Aquarius and **Sagittarius** enjoy each other's company. You also share a love of learning and both need as much intellectual freedom as you can get. This can be a very enduring relationship, whether it's platonic or passionate.

Aquarius and **Capricorn** will give you lots to think about because you'll be so busy trying to work out what makes each other tick. You may never arrive at an answer! You need to find some middle ground and to compromise.

Pisces

Pisces and **Pisces** is wonderful if you're both prepared to face facts rather than pretend your relationship is something it's not. Your life is likely to be highly romantic and you'll love creating a sophisticated home together.

Pisces and **Aries** will be very trying at times. It may also be painful, since your Arien is unlikely to understand how easily you're hurt. Even so, they will encourage you to grow another layer of skin and to laugh at yourself.

Pisces and **Taurus** is a very sensual combination. You'll bring out the romantic in one another, but there will be times when you'll wish your Taurean were less matter-of-fact, practical and sensible.

Pisces and **Gemini** can have fun together but it's awfully easy for you to feel hurt by your Gemini's glib turns of phrase. You may be happier as friends than lovers because your emotional needs are so different.

Pisces and **Cancer** is super because you both express love in the same way. It's wonderful being with someone who takes such care of you, although your Cancerian may not understand your need to be left alone sometimes.

Pisces and **Leo** find it hard to understand each other. At times you may find your Leo rather grand. You share a pronounced artistic streak and you're both very affectionate, but is that enough to keep you together?

Pisces and **Virgo** can be difficult for you. Your Virgo may trample all over your feelings in their well-meaning efforts to point out your faults and help you to rise above them. It all sounds like a lot of unnecessary criticism to you.

Pisces and **Libra** can be incredibly romantic. You could easily have a heady affair straight out of a Hollywood weepie, but staying together is another matter. You may drift apart because you're reluctant to face up to problems.

Pisces and **Scorpio** is a highly emotional and complex pairing. You're both very deep and sensitive, and it may take a while before you begin to understand each other. Once that happens, you won't look back.

Pisces and **Sagittarius** is dicey because you won't know what to make of your forthright Sagittarian. Why are they so blunt? Can't they see that it upsets you? You may be better as friends who share lots of exploits.

Pisces and **Capricorn** is fine if your Capricorn is happy to show their feelings. But if they're buttoned up or repressed, you won't know how to get through to them. Even so, you'll love the way they provide for you.

Pisces and **Aquarius** may as well be talking different languages for all the sense you make to each other. They enjoy talking about ideas that leave you baffled but will struggle to express their emotions in the way you need.

🐏 Aries

Aries and **Aries** is a very energetic combination, and you encourage each other in many different ways. Your relationship is competitive, sexy, exciting and sometimes pretty tempestuous!

Aries and **Taurus** can be difficult because you don't always understand each other. You love your Taurean's loyalty and affection but can feel frustrated if they're a great traditionalist or very stubborn.

Aries and **Gemini** get on like a house on fire and love hatching up new schemes together. But your differing sexual needs could cause problems, especially if your Gemini doesn't share your high sex drive.

Aries and **Cancer** is fine if your Cancerian will give you lots of personal freedom. However, they may be hurt if you aren't at home as much as they'd like, and they'll wonder what you're up to while you're away.

Aries and **Leo** really hit it off well and you'll have a lot of fun together. Sometimes you may wish your Leo would unbend a bit and be less dignified, but you adore the way they love and cherish you. It's great for your ego!

Aries and **Virgo** can be tricky because you have so little in common. You like to rush through life taking each day as it comes while they prefer to plan things in advance and then worry if they're doing the right thing. Irritating!

Aries and **Libra** have a lot to learn from each other. You enjoy the odd skirmish while your Libran prefers to keep the peace. Try to compromise over your differences rather than make them either/or situations.

Aries and **Scorpio** can be very dynamic and sexy together. Power is a huge aphrodisiac for you both so you're greatly attracted to each other. If you're a flirtatious Aries, your Scorpio will soon clip your wings.

Aries and **Sagittarius** are really excited by each other's company. You both adore challenges and will spur one another on to further feats and adventures. Your sex life is lively and interesting, and will keep you pretty busy.

Aries and **Capricorn** may not seem to have much in common on the surface. Yet you are both ambitious and will enjoy watching each other's progress. Sexually, things are surprisingly highly charged and naughty.

Aries and **Aquarius** have a lot of fun together but also share plenty of sparring matches. You get on better as friends than lovers because your Aquarian may not be nearly as interested in sex as you are.

Aries and **Pisces** is one of those tricky combinations that needs a lot of care if it's to succeed. It's horribly easy for you to upset your Piscean, often without realizing it, and you may get bored with having to reassure them so much.

 **Taurus**

Taurus and **Taurus** is great because you're with someone who understands you inside out. Yet although this is comforting at first, it might start to become rather boring after a while, especially if you both like playing it safe.

Taurus and **Gemini** is good for keeping you on your toes, although you may find this tiring in the long term. They need a lot of change and variety, which can unsettle you and make you cling to stability and tradition.

Taurus and **Cancer** is lovely. You both appreciate the same sorts of things in life, such as good food, a loving partner and a cosy home. Once you get together you'll feel as though you've found your true soulmate.

Taurus and **Leo** share a love of luxury and the good things in life. You also know you can trust your Leo to be faithful and loyal, and in return you will shower them with plenty of admiration and moral support.

Taurus and **Virgo** is a very practical combination. Neither of you likes wasting time or money, although you may sometimes wish that your Virgo could be a little less austere and a bit more relaxed. But you still love them.

Taurus and **Libra** can have a very sensual and loving relationship. Neither of you likes conflict and you both need affectionate partners. But you may end up spending a lot of money together on all sorts of luxuries.

Taurus and **Scorpio** is a very powerful combination, especially in the bedroom. You both place a lot of importance on fidelity and loyalty, and you'll both believe that your relationship is the most important thing in your lives.

Taurus and **Sagittarius** don't really understand each other. You enjoy your home comforts and are generally content with life, while your Sagittarian always finds the grass is greener on the other side of the fence.

Taurus and **Capricorn** have a lot in common. You're both lusty, earthy and full of common sense. If you aren't careful, your relationship could get bogged down in practicalities, making you neglect the fun side of things.

Taurus and **Aquarius** struggle to appreciate each other. You enjoy sticking to the status quo whenever possible, while your

Aquarian is always thinking of the future. You're both very stubborn, so rows can end in stalemate.

Taurus and **Pisces** is fine if your Piscean has their feet on the ground, because then you'll enjoy their sensitivity. But if they're very vague or other-worldly, you'll soon get annoyed and lose patience with them.

Taurus and **Aries** isn't the easiest combination for you. Although you enjoy your Arien's enthusiasm, it can wear a bit thin sometimes, especially when they're keen on something that you think is unrealistic or too costly.

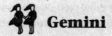

Gemini

Gemini and **Gemini** can be great fun or one big headache. You both crave variety and busy lives, but if you're both very sociable you may rarely see each other. Your sex life may also fizzle out over time.

Gemini and **Cancer** is tricky if you're lovers rather than friends. Although you'll adore your Cancerian's displays of affection at first, after a while they may seem rather clingy or will make you feel trapped.

Gemini and **Leo** have lots of fun together. You genuinely like and love one another, although you may secretly be amused sometimes by your Leo's regal behaviour and want to give them some gentle teasing.

Gemini and **Virgo** hit it off surprisingly well. There's so much for you to talk about and plenty of scope for having a good laugh. You're tremendous friends, whether your relationship is sexual or purely platonic.

Gemini and **Libra** is one of the most enjoyable combinations of all for you. You can encourage your easy-going Libran to be more assertive while they help you to relax, and also bring out the romance in your soul.

Gemini and **Scorpio** make uncomfortable bedfellows but good friends. You have very little in common sexually but are intrigued by each other's minds. You share an insatiable curiosity about human nature.

Gemini and **Sagittarius** have a really good time together. You especially enjoy learning new things from one another and never run out of things to talk about. Travel and books are just two of your many shared enthusiasms.

Gemini and **Capricorn** isn't very easy because you're so different. At first you're intrigued by your Capricorn's responsibility and common sense, but after a while they may seem a little staid or stuffy for you.

Gemini and **Aquarius** are fantastic friends. You're used to having the upper hand intellectually with people but here is someone who makes you think and encourages you to look at life in a new way.

Gemini and **Pisces** can be tricky because it's easy to hurt your Piscean's feelings without even realizing it. Neither of you is very keen on facing up to harsh reality, which causes problems if you both avoid dealing with the facts.

Gemini and **Aries** is tremendous fun and you'll spend a lot of time laughing. If even half the plans you make come to fruition, you'll have a fantastic time together with never a dull moment.

Gemini and **Taurus** can make you wonder what you're doing wrong. Your Taurean may seem bemused or even slightly alarmed by you, and positively threatened by your need for as much variety in your life as possible.

Compatibility in Love and Sex at a glance

F / M	♈	♉	♊	♋	♌	♍	♎	♏	♐	♑	♒	♓
♈	8	5	9	7	9	4	7	8	9	7	7	3
♉	6	8	4	10	7	8	8	7	3	8	2	8
♊	8	2	7	3	8	7	9	4	9	4	9	4
♋	5	10	4	8	6	5	6	8	2	9	2	8
♌	9	8	9	7	7	4	9	6	8	7	9	6
♍	4	8	6	4	4	7	6	7	7	9	4	4
♎	7	8	10	7	8	5	9	6	9	6	10	6
♏	7	9	4	7	6	6	7	10	5	6	5	7
♐	9	4	10	4	9	7	8	4	9	6	9	5
♑	7	8	4	9	6	8	6	4	4	8	4	5
♒	8	6	9	4	9	4	9	6	8	7	8	2
♓	7	6	7	9	6	7	6	9	7	5	4	9

1 = the pits
10 = the peaks

Key

♈ – Aries
♉ – Taurus
♊ – Gemini
♋ – Cancer
♌ – Leo
♍ – Virgo

♎ – Libra
♏ – Scorpio
♐ – Sagittarius
♑ – Capricorn
♒ – Aquarius
♓ – Pisces

Compatibility in Friendship at a glance

F M	♈	♉	♊	♋	♌	♍	♎	♏	♐	♑	♒	♓
♈	8	5	10	5	9	3	7	8	9	6	8	5
♉	6	9	6	10	7	8	7	6	4	9	3	9
♊	9	3	9	4	9	8	10	5	10	5	10	6
♋	6	9	4	9	5	4	6	9	4	10	3	9
♌	10	7	9	6	9	4	8	6	9	6	9	7
♍	5	9	8	4	9	8	5	8	8	10	5	6
♎	8	9	10	8	8	6	9	5	9	6	10	7
♏	7	8	5	8	7	7	6	9	4	5	6	8
♐	9	5	10	4	10	8	8	4	10	7	9	6
♑	6	9	5	10	6	9	5	5	4	9	5	6
♒	9	6	10	5	9	5	9	7	9	5	9	3
♓	6	7	6	10	6	8	7	9	8	6	4	10

1 = the pits
10 = the peaks

Key

♈ – Aries
♉ – Taurus
♊ – Gemini
♋ – Cancer
♌ – Leo
♍ – Virgo

♎ – Libra
♏ – Scorpio
♐ – Sagittarius
♑ – Capricorn
♒ – Aquarius
♓ – Pisces

FAMILY AND FRIENDS

What does your Sun sign say about your relationship with your family and friends? Do you value family far above friends, or do you have the sort of family that makes you glad you can choose your friends? Read on to discover how you relate to those important people in your life.

🦀 Cancer

If you're a typical Cancerian, your friends and family mean the world to you. You may not even have many friends; you may spend so much time with your family that you don't feel the need for anyone else in your life. In turn, you may be slightly offended when members of the family have outside interests because you think they shouldn't need them. Blood is definitely thicker than water, as far as you're concerned. If you don't get on well with your relatives or you're separated from them for some reason, you'll create your own family group from friends and colleagues. You're very warm and caring, and are always concerned about other people's welfare. Sometimes this can seem rather claustrophobic to others, even though you're doing it from the best of motives. So try to avoid smother love!

 Leo

You're very family-minded and you love surrounding yourself with all your nearest and dearest. You adore being with children and will pay a lot of attention to their upbringing, encouraging them to express themselves and be creative. Yet you are also a stickler for good manners so will teach them to behave properly and not let you down. You're strict when you think the occasion demands it but try to be as loving and affectionate as possible. Friends are another essential part of your life and you enjoy making a big fuss of them. You place a lot of importance on loyalty and trust, and will be bitterly hurt if a loved one betrays you or is harshly critical of you. You may forgive them once or twice, but it will be a different story if they continue to do it.

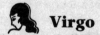 **Virgo**

It may not always be easy for you to show your feelings but that doesn't mean you don't have them. You can be very loving and affectionate, but you often aren't very demonstrative. In fact, you can feel quite uncomfortable when you're with people who are very lovey-dovey because it just isn't your style. You're very discriminating, even with close members of the family, so you may find that you love them but don't really like them very much. If you aren't keen on a relative, you'll be polite but will try to restrict the amount of time you spend with them. When it comes to friends, you choose them wisely and well. You won't squander your affections and are unlikely to be chums with anyone who's boring, lousy company or a complete numbskull.

Libra

Harmonious relationships are essential to your well-being, no matter who they're with. It's important to you that you get on as well with your family as your friends, and you'll feel quite churned up when you have a disagreement with anyone. You don't enjoy spending a lot of time on your own, so you'll like it if your family can give you plenty of company. You'll do your best to instil courtesy and good manners in your children. When choosing your friends, you're attracted to people who are bright, witty and great company. It's very easy for you to make friends because you're naturally so charming and outgoing. The difficulty for you may be in managing to keep up with all your chums because you've got so many of them.

Scorpio

As with every other area of your life, you take your relationships with your friends and family very seriously. You may not be enamoured with all your family but you will treat them with respect and consideration, hoping that they'll never guess your real feelings about them. Yet you'll be ultra-loyal to the members of your family that you really care about, and they'll know that they can rely on you completely when the chips are down. When you have children, you dote on them but you're very strict with them too. As for friends, you tend to make them for life. You may still be in touch with friends you made when you were very young. However, if someone betrays you or seriously displeases you, you will sever all connection with them if needs be and never give them another chance.

Sagittarius

You're so outgoing and gregarious that you can't imagine not having lots of friends. They probably come from many different walks of life and cultures because you aren't interested in race, religion, sexuality or any of the other social divisions that tend to separate people. However, you won't spend much time with anyone who is narrow-minded or deeply negative, and they also won't be a boon companion if they've got fluff for brains. When it comes to your relatives, you like seeing them but they aren't the be-all and end-all of your existence. It's a different story if you have children, because you'll lavish tremendous amounts of love and energy on them, and will adore teaching them all about the world. If you can transmit some of your optimism and enthusiasm to them, you'll be very pleased with yourself.

Capricorn

Blood ties mean a lot to you and it will be a source of great sadness if you aren't as close to your family as you would like. Even so, you will do your best to keep in touch with everyone because, deep down, you believe that stable families are the bedrock of society. When bringing up your own family you will do your best to teach your children to respect their elders, and will be happiest with a traditional family unit. If you are separated from your family, you will establish a strong network of friends who feel like family or the next best thing. You're a very faithful, loving and dependable friend, although you're a lot more sensitive than people may think. You don't wear your heart on your sleeve but you're still easily hurt.

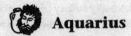

Aquarius

Friendship is one of your greatest gifts. You excel at making friends and you attract people from all walks of life and all ages. You can see nothing odd about a forty-year age gap between friends, nor are you interested in choosing influential or wealthy friends because of what they might be able to give you. If you like someone, you like them, and that's all there is to it. This can sometimes cause problems if your partner doesn't understand or is jealous because they consider your best friend to be competition for their affections. As far as family are concerned, you enjoy seeing them every now and then but aren't overly family-minded. You make a point of keeping in regular contact with the relatives you like but aren't too worried if you can't see much of the others.

 **Pisces**

You enjoy developing strong family ties because you like the sense of continuity it gives you. It's great to be with people who you've known for most, if not all, of your life. You would be very fortunate if all your relatives were lovable and likeable, but you do your best to tolerate the ones who you aren't so keen on. You lavish a lot of love on the ones who are your favourites, and will find ways to let them know that you think they're special. Yet you're so sensitive to the plight of lame ducks that you'll feel sorry for the people you don't like, probably because you realize they aren't very popular with anyone. You choose your friends carefully, preferring people who are on your emotional wavelength and who share your view of the world.

 Aries

Being born under the sign of Aries makes you affectionate, enthusiastic and impulsive, and you bring all these qualities into your relationships with family and friends. You adore children and make a special effort to get on well with them. You're perfectly happy romping around on the floor with them or taking them on long walks and teaching them about nature. You're always prepared to think the best of people and you're ready to give them the benefit of the doubt if there are any questions about their behaviour. You are essentially trusting, which means you can be badly hurt when people betray that trust. Yet you don't seem to learn from your mistakes and you're quite likely to do the same things all over again, telling yourself that this time it will be different. When it isn't, you're very disappointed.

Taurus

Your family mean the world to you and you'll do whatever you can to support them. Part of this support means providing for their daily needs, so you're perfectly prepared to work round the clock if that's what it takes to feed and clothe them. You are also extremely loyal and steadfast, so loved ones know they can count on you to be there when they need you. In return, you need to be loved and appreciated. Sometimes, an element of possessiveness may creep into the equation, making you treat your loved ones as though they're your personal belongings. For instance, you may secretly feel as though you've been supplanted when your children are old enough to fall in love, or you might be rather worried if your friends don't spend as much time with you as you'd like. If you relax, you'll realize that there's more than enough love to go round.

Gemini

As one of the most sociable signs in the zodiac, you have an instinctive need for kindred spirits in your life. You need people to bounce ideas off and to chat to, and you won't really care if they're friends or family if you like them. For instance, you may be best friends with your cousin, knowing that you would have liked him or her even if you weren't related. You enjoy keeping up with the latest gossip about all the people in your life, so family occasions can be great fun for you because you're able to find out what's going on. Children are strongly attracted to you because they sense your own childlike nature, and you'll happily spend hours playing with them or reading to them. When you're away from family and friends, you'll do your best to keep in touch with them by phone, letter or e-mail.

BORN ON THE CUSP?

Were you born on the cusp of Cancer – at the beginning or end of the sign? If so, you may have spent years wondering which sign you belong to. Are you a Cancerian, a Gemini or a Leo? Different horoscope books and columns can give different dates for when the Sun moves into each sign, leaving you utterly confused. Yet none of these dates is wrong, as you'll discover in a minute. Checking your birth date, and time if you know it, in the list given in this chapter will allow you to solve the mystery at long last!

Many people believe that the Sun moves like clockwork from one sign to another on a specific day each year. But this isn't always true. For instance, let's look at the dates for the sign of Cancer. On the cover of this book I give them as 22 June to 22 July. Very often, the Sun will obediently change signs on these days but sometimes it won't. It can move from Gemini into Cancer on 21 or 22 June and it can move into Leo on 22 or 23 July.

So how can you find out which sign you belong to if you were born on the cusp of Cancer? The only information you need is the place, year, day and the time of your birth if you know it. It helps to have the time of birth because if the Sun did move signs on your birthday, you can see whether it moved before or after you were born. If you don't have an exact time, even knowing whether it was morning or after-noon can be a help. For instance, if you were born in the morning and the Sun didn't move signs on your birthday until the afternoon, that will be enough information to tell you which sign is yours.

You need to know the place in case you were born outside the United Kingdom and have to convert its local time zone to British time. This information is easily available in many diaries and reference books.

Four Simple Steps to Find your Sun Sign

1 Write down the year, day, time and place of your birth, in that order.
2 If you were born outside the United Kingdom, you must convert your birth date and time to British time by adding or subtracting the relevant number of hours from your birth time to convert it to British time. This may take your birthday into the following day or back to the previous day. If so, write down this new date and time because that will be the one you use in the following calculations. If summer time was oper-ating you must deduct the relevant number of hours to convert your birth time to Greenwich Mean Time (GMT).
3 If you were born in Britain, look up your year of birth in the list of British Summer Time (BST) changes to see if BST was operating when you were born. If it was, subtract the appropriate number of hours from your birth time to con-vert it to GMT. This may give you a different time and/or date of birth.
4 Look up your year of birth in the Annual Sun Sign Changes list. If you were born within these dates and times, you are a Cancerian. If you were born outside them, you are either a Gemini if you were born in June, or a Leo if you were born in July.

Two Examples

Here are a couple of examples so you can see how the process works. Let's say we're looking for the Sun sign of Mike, who was born in the UK on 22 June 1942 at 01:55. Start by checking the list of British Summer Time dates to see if BST was operating at the time of his birth. It was, but you will see that he was born during a phase when two hours had been added, so you have to subtract two hours from his birth time to convert it to GMT. This gives him a birth time of 23:55 on the previous day – therefore his GMT birthday is 21 June and his GMT birth time is 23:55. Write this down, so you don't forget it. Now turn to the Annual Sun Sign Changes list and look up 1942, his year of birth. In that year, the Sun moved into Cancer on 22 June at 01:17, and Mike's GMT birth was at 23:55 the previous day, so he is a Gemini, not a Cancerian. However, if he had been born on 22 June 1942 at 03:55 (which gives him a GMT birth time of 01:55 on the same day), the Sun would have been in Cancer so he would be a Cancerian.

But what would his sign be if he were born on 23 July 1942 at 15:55? First check the dates in the BST list. You will see he was born during a period when two hours had been added for BST, so you must subtract two hours to convert his birth time to GMT. This changes it to 13:55 on 23 July 1942. Write this down. Now look up the Sun sign dates for 1942 again. This time, look at the July date. The Sun was in Cancer until 23 July at 12:07. So Mike's GMT birth time was after the Sun had moved into Leo, making him a Leo.

Dates for British Summer Time

If your birthday falls within these dates and times, you were born during BST and will have to convert your birth time back to GMT. To do this, subtract one hour from your birth time. If

you were born during a period that is marked *, you must
subtract two hours from your birth time to convert it to GMT.
All times are given in BST, using the 24-hour clock.

1920 28 Mar, 02:00–25 Oct, 01:59 inc	**1950** 16 Apr, 02:00–22 Oct, 01:59 inc
1921 3 Apr, 02:00–3 Oct, 01:59 inc	**1951** 15 Apr, 02:00–21 Oct, 01:59 inc
1922 26 Mar, 02:00–8 Oct, 01:59 inc	**1952** 20 Apr, 02:00–26 Oct, 01:59 inc
1923 22 Apr, 02:00–16 Sep, 01:59 inc	**1953** 19 Apr, 02:00–4 Oct, 01:59 inc
1924 13 Apr, 02:00–21 Sep, 01:59 inc	**1954** 11 Apr, 02:00–3 Oct, 01:59 inc
1925 19 Apr, 02:00–4 Oct, 01:59 inc	**1955** 17 Apr, 02:00–2 Oct, 01:59 inc
1926 18 Apr, 02:00–3 Oct, 01:59 inc	**1956** 22 Apr, 02:00–7 Oct, 01:59 inc
1927 10 Apr, 02:00–2 Oct, 01:59 inc	**1957** 14 Apr, 02:00–6 Oct, 01:59 inc
1928 22 Apr, 02:00–7 Oct, 01:59 inc	**1958** 20 Apr, 02:00–5 Oct, 01:59 inc
1929 21 Apr, 02:00–6 Oct, 01:59 inc	**1959** 19 Apr, 02:00–4 Oct, 01:59 inc
1930 13 Apr, 02:00–5 Oct, 01:59 inc	**1960** 10 Apr, 02:00–2 Oct, 01:59 inc
1931 19 Apr, 02:00–4 Oct, 01:59 inc	**1961** 26 Mar, 02:00–29 Oct, 01:59 inc
1932 17 Apr, 02:00–2 Oct, 01:59 inc	**1962** 25 Mar, 02:00–28 Oct, 01:59 inc
1933 9 Apr, 02:00–8 Oct, 01:59 inc	**1963** 31 Mar, 02:00–27 Oct, 01:59 inc
1934 22 Apr, 02:00–7 Oct, 01:59 inc	**1964** 22 Mar, 02:00–25 Oct, 01:59 inc
1935 14 Apr, 02:00–6 Oct, 01:59 inc	**1965** 21 Mar, 02:00–24 Oct, 01:59 inc
1936 19 Apr, 02:00–4 Oct, 01:59 inc	**1966** 20 Mar, 02:00–23 Oct, 01:59 inc
1937 18 Apr, 02:00–3 Oct, 01:59 inc	**1967** 19 Mar, 02:00–29 Oct, 01:59 inc
1938 10 Apr, 02:00–2 Oct, 01:59 inc	**1968** 18 Feb, 02:00–31 Dec, 23:59 inc
1939 16 Apr, 02:00–19 Nov, 01:59 inc	**1969** 1 Jan, 00:00–31 Dec, 23:59 inc
1940 25 Feb, 02:00–31 Dec, 23:59 inc	**1970** 1 Jan, 00:00–31 Dec, 23:59 inc
1941 1 Jan, 00:00–4 May, 01:59 inc	**1971** 1 Jan, 00:00–31 Oct, 01:59 inc
1941 4 May, 02:00–10 Aug, 01:59 inc*	**1972** 19 Mar, 02:00–29 Oct, 01:59 inc
1941 10 Aug, 02:00–31 Dec, 23:59 inc	**1973** 18 Mar, 02:00–28 Oct, 01:59 inc
1942 1 Jan, 00:00–5 Apr, 01:59 inc	**1974** 17 Mar, 02:00–27 Oct, 01:59 inc
1942 5 Apr, 02:00–9 Aug, 01:59 inc*	**1975** 16 Mar, 02:00–26 Oct, 01:59 inc
1942 9 Aug, 02:00–31 Dec, 23:59 inc	**1976** 21 Mar, 02:00–24 Oct, 01:59 inc
1943 1 Jan, 00:00–4 Apr, 01:59 inc	**1977** 20 Mar, 02:00–23 Oct, 01:59 inc
1943 4 Apr, 02:00–15 Aug, 01:59 inc*	**1978** 19 Mar, 02:00–29 Oct, 01:59 inc
1943 15 Aug, 02:00–31 Dec, 23:59 inc	**1979** 18 Mar, 02:00–28 Oct, 01:59 inc
1944 1 Jan, 00:00–2 Apr, 01:59 inc	**1980** 16 Mar, 02:00–26 Oct, 01:59 inc
1944 2 Apr, 02:00–17 Sep, 01:59 inc*	**1981** 29 Mar, 01:00–25 Oct, 00:59 inc
1944 17 Sep, 02:00–31 Dec, 23:59 inc	**1982** 28 Mar, 01:00–24 Oct, 00:59 inc
1945 1 Jan, 02:00–2 Apr, 01:59 inc	**1983** 27 Mar, 01:00–23 Oct, 00:59 inc
1945 2 Apr, 02:00–15 Jul, 01:59 inc*	**1984** 25 Mar, 01:00–28 Oct, 00:59 inc
1945 15 Jul, 02:00–7 Oct, 01:59 inc	**1985** 31 Mar, 01:00–27 Oct, 00:59 inc
1946 14 Apr, 02:00–6 Oct, 01:59 inc	**1986** 30 Mar, 01:00–26 Oct, 00:59 inc
1947 16 Mar, 02:00–13 Apr, 01:59 inc	**1987** 29 Mar, 01:00–25 Oct, 00:59 inc
1947 13 Apr, 02:00–10 Aug, 01:59 inc*	**1988** 27 Mar, 01:00–23 Oct, 00:59 inc
1947 10 Aug, 02:00–2 Nov, 01:59 inc	**1989** 26 Mar, 01:00–29 Oct, 00:59 inc
1948 14 Mar, 02:00–31 Oct, 01:59 inc	**1990** 25 Mar, 01:00–28 Oct, 00:59 inc
1949 3 Apr, 02:00–30 Oct, 01:59 inc	**1991** 31 Mar, 01:00–27 Oct, 00:59 inc

1992 29 Mar, 01:00–25 Oct, 00:59 inc
1993 28 Mar, 01:00–24 Oct, 00:59 inc
1994 27 Mar, 01:00–23 Oct, 00:59 inc
1995 26 Mar, 01:00–22 Oct, 00:59 inc
1996 31 Mar, 01:00–27 Oct, 00:59 inc
1997 30 Mar, 01:00–26 Oct, 00:59 inc

1998 29 Mar, 01:00–25 Oct, 00:59 inc
1999 28 Mar, 01:00–31 Oct, 00:59 inc
2000 26 Mar, 01:00–29 Oct, 00:59 inc
2001 25 Mar, 01:00–28 Oct, 00:59 inc
2002 31 Mar, 01:00–27 Oct, 00:59 inc
2003 30 Mar, 01:00–26 Oct, 00:59 inc

* Subtract two hours from the birth time to convert it to GMT.

Annual Sun Sign Changes

If your birthday falls within these dates and times, you are a Cancerian. If you were born in June before the first date and time, you are a Gemini. If you were born in July after the second date and time, you are a Leo. All times are given in GMT, using the 24-hour clock.

1920 21 Jun, 17:40–23 Jul, 04:34 inc
1921 21 Jun, 23:36–23 Jul, 10:30 inc
1922 22 Jun, 05:27–23 Jul, 16:19 inc
1923 22 Jun, 11:03–23 Jul, 22:00 inc
1924 21 Jun, 17:00–23 Jul, 03:57 inc
1925 21 Jun, 22:50–23 Jul, 09:44 inc
1926 22 Jun, 04:30–23 Jul, 15:24 inc
1927 22 Jun, 10:23–23 Jul, 21:16 inc
1928 21 Jun, 16:07–23 Jul, 03:02 inc
1929 21 Jun, 22:01–23 Jul, 08:53 inc
1930 22 Jun, 03:53–23 Jul, 14:41 inc
1931 22 Jun, 09:28–23 Jul, 20:21 inc
1932 21 Jun, 15:23–23 Jul, 02:17 inc
1933 21 Jun, 21:12–23 Jul, 08:05 inc
1934 22 Jun, 02:48–23 Jul, 13:42 inc
1935 22 Jun, 08:38–23 Jul, 19:32 inc
1936 21 Jun, 14:22–23 Jul, 01:17 inc
1937 21 Jun, 20:12–23 Jul, 07:06 inc
1938 22 Jun, 02:04–23 Jul, 12:57 inc
1939 22 Jun, 07:40–23 Jul, 18:36 inc
1940 21 Jun, 13:37–23 Jul, 00:34 inc
1941 21 Jun, 19:34–23 Jul, 06:26 inc
1942 22 Jun, 01:17–23 Jul, 12:07 inc
1943 22 Jun, 07:13–23 Jul, 18:04 inc
1944 21 Jun, 13:03–22 Jul, 23:55 inc
1945 21 Jun, 18:53–23 Jul, 05:45 inc

1946 22 Jun, 00:45–23 Jul, 11:37 inc
1947 22 Jun, 06:19–23 Jul, 17:14 inc
1948 21 Jun, 12:11–22 Jul, 23:07 inc
1949 21 Jun, 18:03–23 Jul, 04:56 inc
1950 21 Jun, 23:37–23 Jul, 10:29 inc
1951 22 Jun, 05:25–23 Jul, 16:20 inc
1952 21 Jun, 11:13–22 Jul, 22:07 inc
1953 21 Jun, 17:00–23 Jul, 03:52 inc
1954 21 Jun, 22:55–23 Jul, 09:44 inc
1955 22 Jun, 04:32–23 Jul, 15:24 inc
1956 21 Jun, 10:24–22 Jul, 21:19 inc
1957 21 Jun, 16:21–23 Jul, 03:14 inc
1958 21 Jun, 21:57–23 Jul, 08:50 inc
1959 22 Jun, 03:50–23 Jul, 14:45 inc
1960 21 Jun, 09:43–22 Jul, 20:37 inc
1961 21 Jun, 15:31–23 Jul, 02:23 inc
1962 21 Jun, 21:25–23 Jul, 08:18 inc
1963 22 Jun, 03:05–23 Jul, 13:59 inc
1964 21 Jun, 08:57–22 Jul, 19:52 inc
1965 21 Jun, 14:56–23 Jul, 01:48 inc
1966 21 Jun, 20:34–23 Jul, 07:23 inc
1967 22 Jun, 02:23–23 Jul, 13:15 inc
1968 21 Jun, 08:14–22 Jul, 19:07 inc
1969 21 Jun, 13:56–23 Jul, 00:48 inc
1970 21 Jun, 19:43–23 Jul, 06:37 inc
1971 22 Jun, 01:20–23 Jul, 12:14 inc

1972 21 Jun, 07:07–22 Jul, 18:02 inc
1973 21 Jun, 13:01–22 Jul, 23:55 inc
1974 21 Jun, 18:38–23 Jul, 05:30 inc
1975 22 Jun, 00:27–23 Jul, 11:22 inc
1976 21 Jun, 06:25–22 Jul, 17:18 inc
1977 21 Jun, 12:15–22 Jul, 23:03 inc
1978 21 Jun, 18:10–23 Jul, 05:00 inc
1979 21 Jun, 23:57–23 Jul, 10:48 inc
1980 21 Jun, 05:48–22 Jul, 16:42 inc
1981 21 Jun, 11:46–22 Jul, 22:40 inc
1982 21 Jun, 17:24–23 Jul, 04:15 inc
1983 21 Jun, 23:10–23 Jul, 10:04 inc
1984 21 Jun, 05:03–22 Jul, 15:58 inc
1985 21 Jun, 10:45–22 Jul, 21:36 inc
1986 21 Jun, 16:31–23 Jul, 03:24 inc
1987 21 Jun, 22:12–23 Jul, 09:06 inc

1988 21 Jun, 03:57–22 Jul, 14:51 inc
1989 21 Jun, 09:54–22 Jul, 20:45 inc
1990 21 Jun, 15:34–23 Jul, 02:21 inc
1991 21 Jun, 21:20–23 Jul, 08:11 inc
1992 21 Jun, 03:15–22 Jul, 14:09 inc
1993 21 Jun, 09:01–22 Jul, 19:51 inc
1994 21 Jun, 14:49–23 Jul, 01:41 inc
1995 21 Jun, 20:35–23 Jul, 07:30 inc
1996 21 Jun, 02:25–22 Jul, 13:19 inc
1997 21 Jun, 08:21–22 Jul, 19:15 inc
1998 21 Jun, 14:04–23 Jul, 00:55 inc
1999 21 Jun, 19:50–23 Jul, 06:44 inc
2000 21 Jun, 01:49–22 Jul, 12:43 inc
2001 21 Jun, 07:39–22 Jul, 18:26 inc
2002 21 Jun, 13:25–23 Jul, 00:15 inc
2003 21 Jun, 19:12–23 Jul, 06:04 inc